UNDERCOVER COMBAT
COURAGEOUS SPIES OF WORLD WAR I

BY MATTHEW K. MANNING

ILLUSTRATED BY LEO TRINIDAD

CAPSTONE PRESS
a capstone imprint

Published by Capstone Press, an imprint of Capstone.
1710 Roe Crest Drive
North Mankato, Minnesota 56003
capstonepub.com

Copyright © 2025 by Capstone. All rights reserved. No part of this publication may be reproduced in whole or in part, or stored in a retrieval system, or transmitted in any form or by any means, electronic, mechanical, photocopying, recording, or otherwise, without written permission of the publisher.

Library of Congress Cataloging-in-Publication data is available on the Library of Congress website.

ISBN: 9781669085607 (hardcover)
ISBN: 9781669085775 (paperback)
ISBN: 9781669085591 (ebook PDF)

Summary: A young British officer starts a spy base disguised as a shipping company. A German naval engineer turns against his country to aid the Allies. A Frenchwoman leads a spy network that saves thousands of British soldiers. These gripping, true stories of espionage shifted the course of World War I. What drove these courageous spies to risk their lives in the deadly game of war intelligence?

Editorial Credits:
Editor: Donald Lemke; Designer: Kay Fraser;
Production Specialist: Katy LaVigne

Any additional websites and resources referenced in this book are not maintained, authorized, or sponsored by Capstone. All product and company names are trademarks™ or registered® trademarks of their respective holders.

TABLE OF CONTENTS

INTRODUCTION
THE GREAT WAR 4

CHAPTER ONE
LOUISE DE BETTIGNIES: THE ALICE NETWORK 6

CHAPTER TWO
RICHARD B. TINSLEY: SPY TO A "T" 22

CHAPTER THREE
SYLVANUS MORLEY: DIGGING FOR INFORMATION 32

INTRODUCTION

THE GREAT WAR

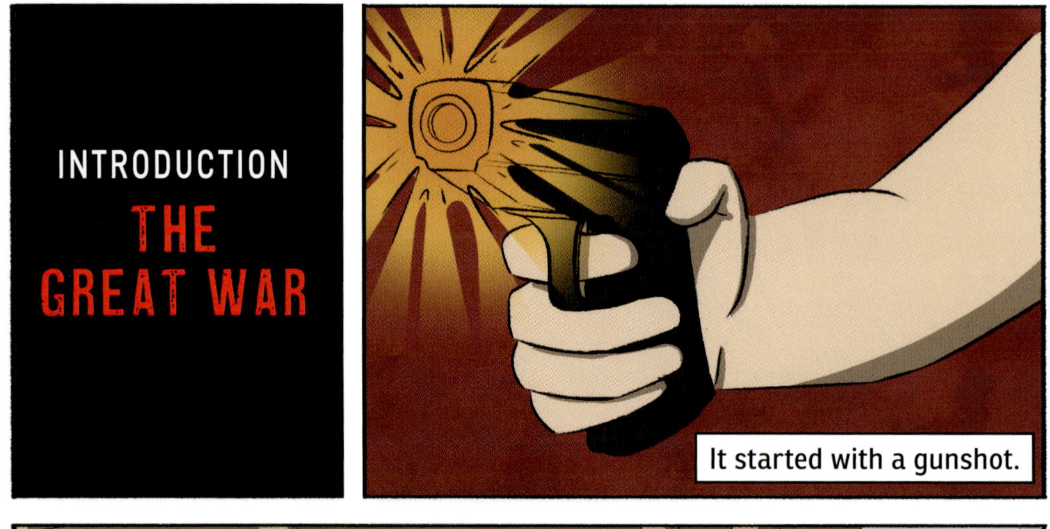

It started with a gunshot.

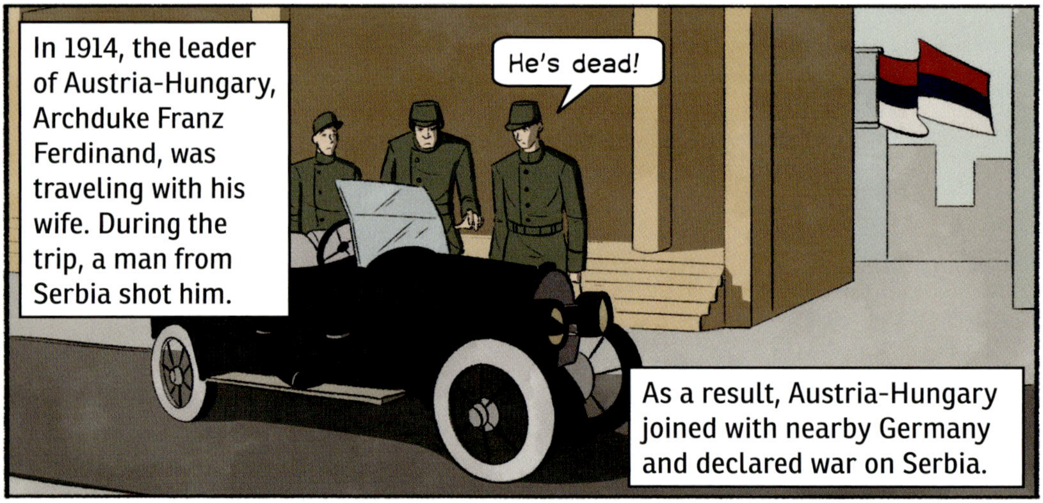

In 1914, the leader of Austria-Hungary, Archduke Franz Ferdinand, was traveling with his wife. During the trip, a man from Serbia shot him.
He's dead!
As a result, Austria-Hungary joined with nearby Germany and declared war on Serbia.

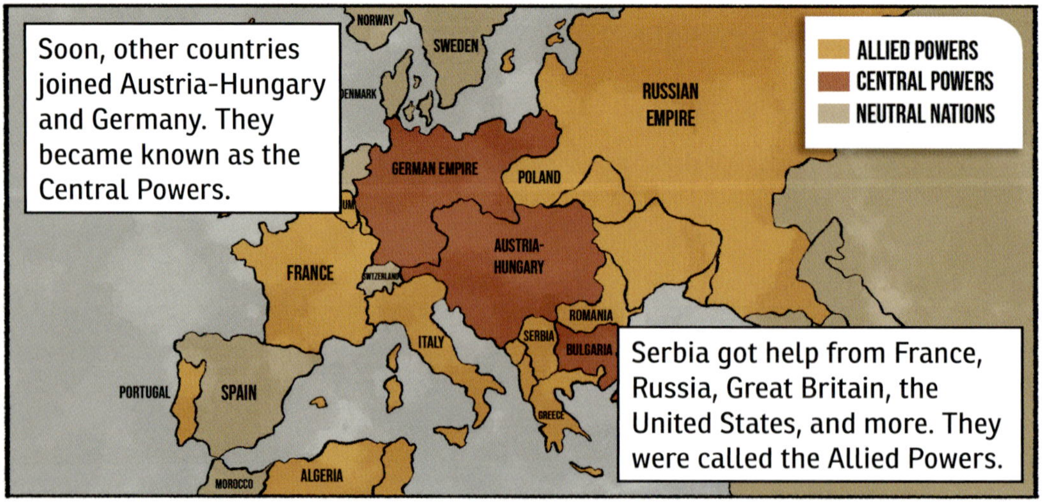

Soon, other countries joined Austria-Hungary and Germany. They became known as the Central Powers.
ALLIED POWERS
CENTRAL POWERS
NEUTRAL NATIONS
NORWAY
SWEDEN
RUSSIAN EMPIRE
GERMAN EMPIRE
POLAND
AUSTRIA-HUNGARY
FRANCE
ITALY
ROMANIA
SERBIA
BULGARIA
GREECE
PORTUGAL
SPAIN
MOROCCO
ALGERIA
Serbia got help from France, Russia, Great Britain, the United States, and more. They were called the Allied Powers.

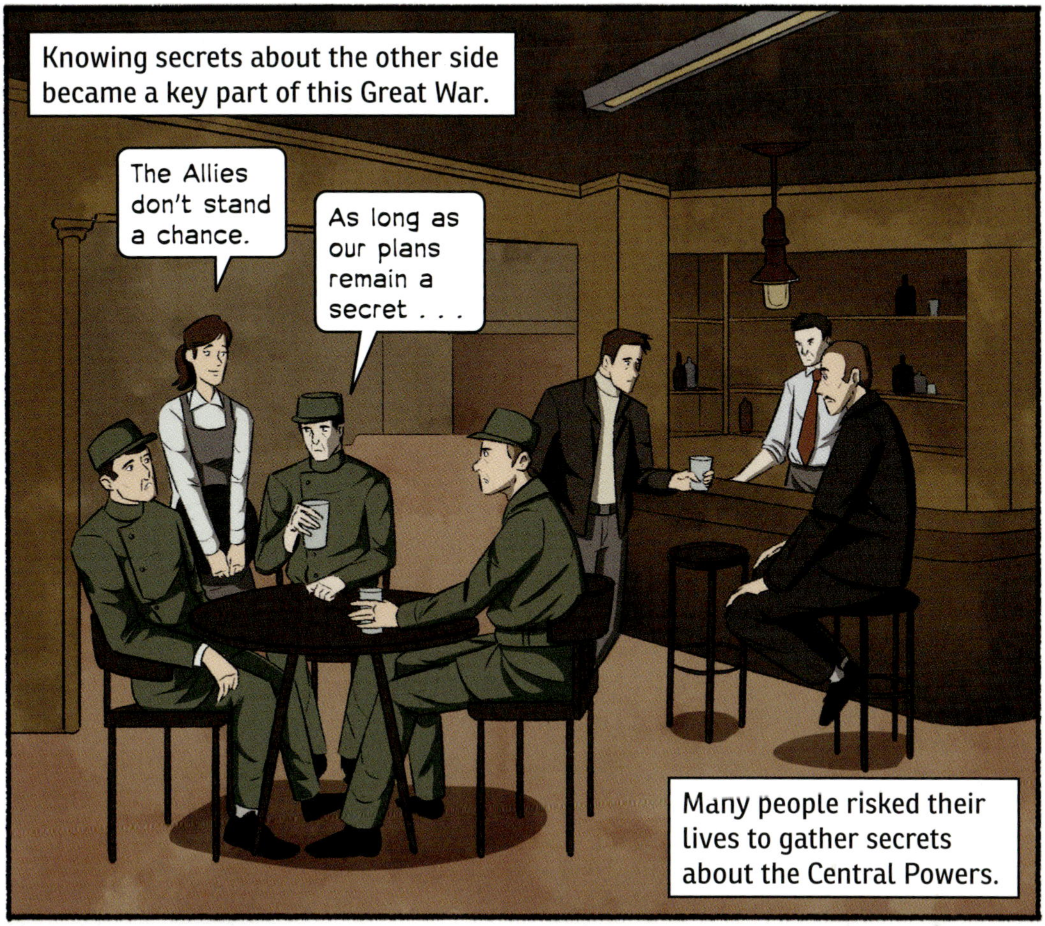
Knowing secrets about the other side became a key part of this Great War.
The Allies don't stand a chance.
As long as our plans remain a secret . . .
Many people risked their lives to gather secrets about the Central Powers.

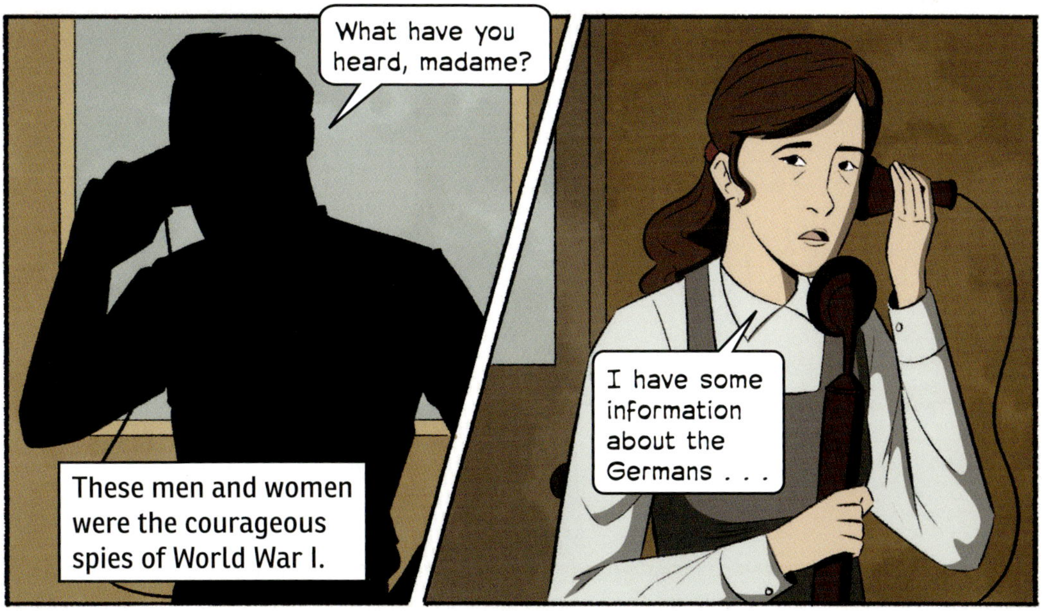
What have you heard, madame?
I have some information about the Germans . . .
These men and women were the courageous spies of World War I.

CHAPTER ONE

LOUISE DE BETTIGNIES: THE ALICE NETWORK

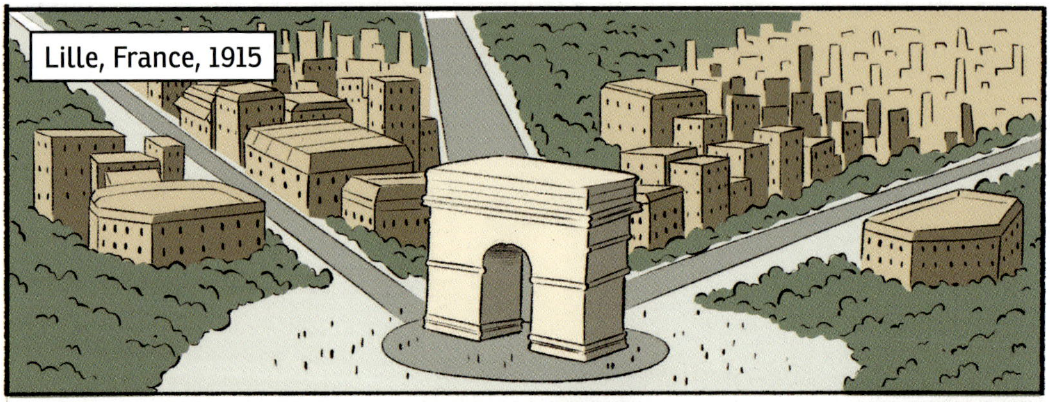
Lille, France, 1915

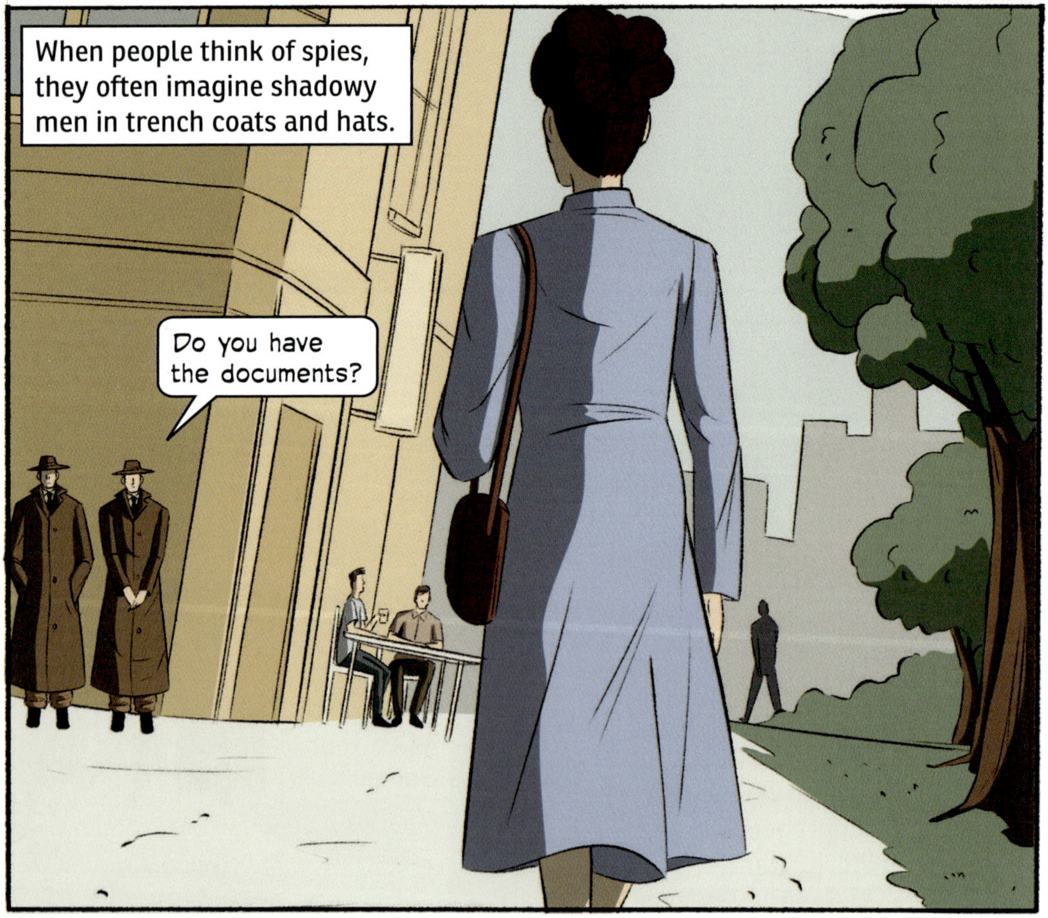
When people think of spies, they often imagine shadowy men in trench coats and hats.
Do you have the documents?

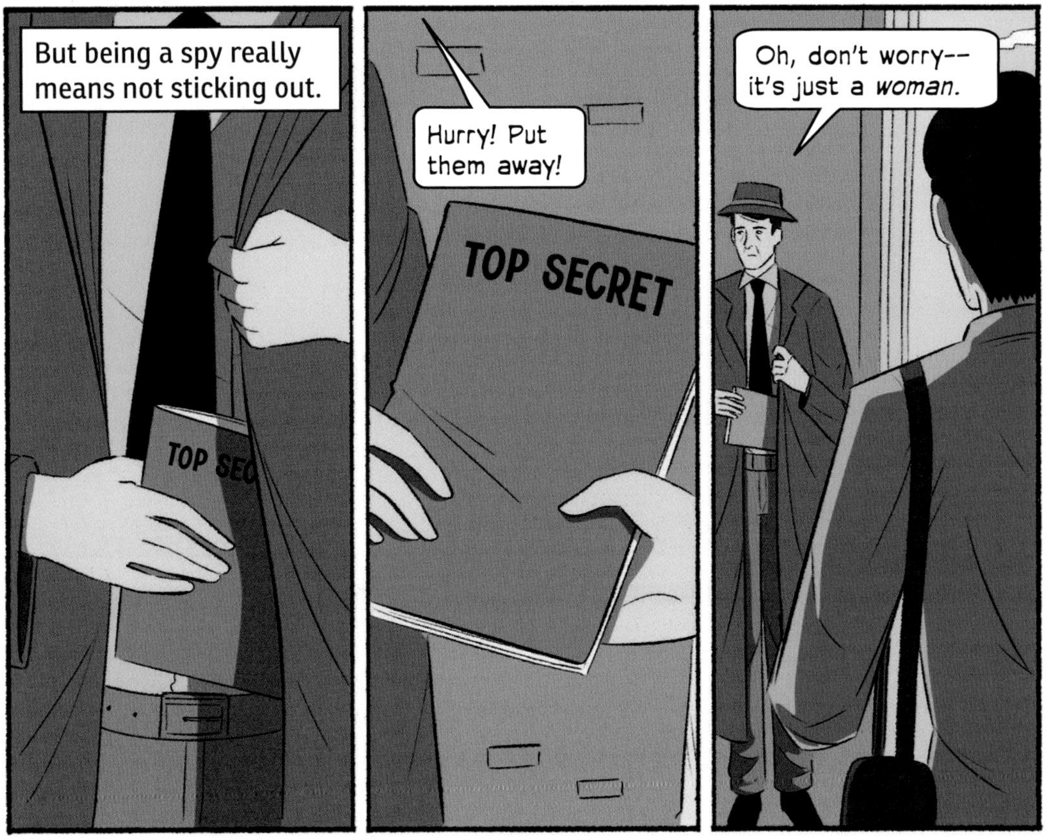
But being a spy really means not sticking out.
TOP SEC
Hurry! Put them away!
TOP SECRET
Oh, don't worry-- it's just a *woman.*

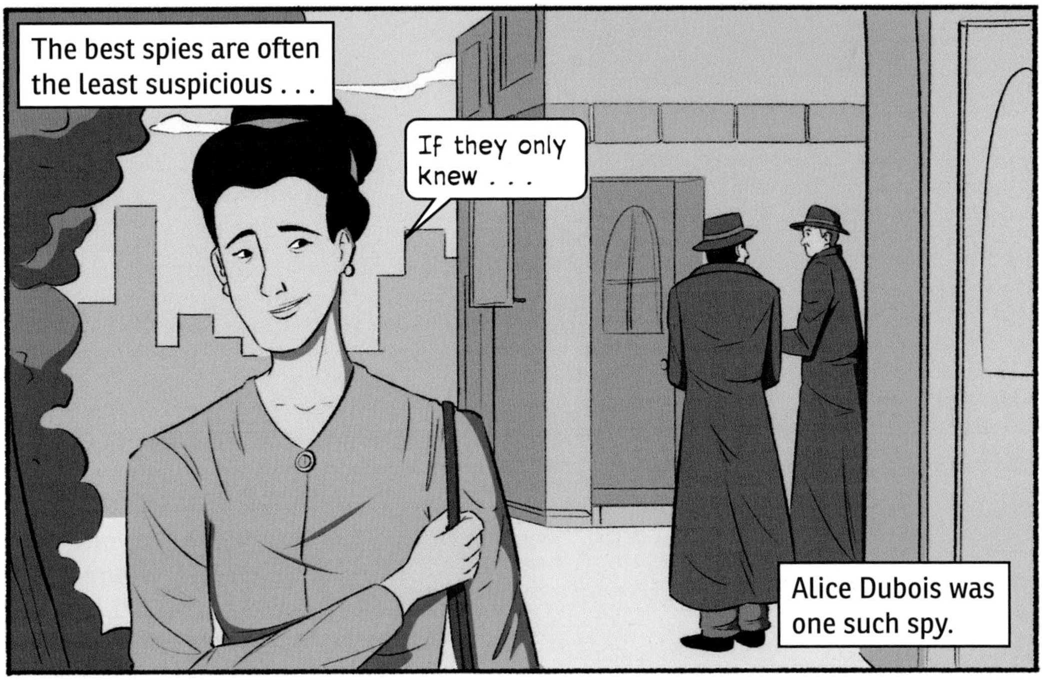
The best spies are often the least suspicious . . .
If they only knew . . .
Alice Dubois was one such spy.

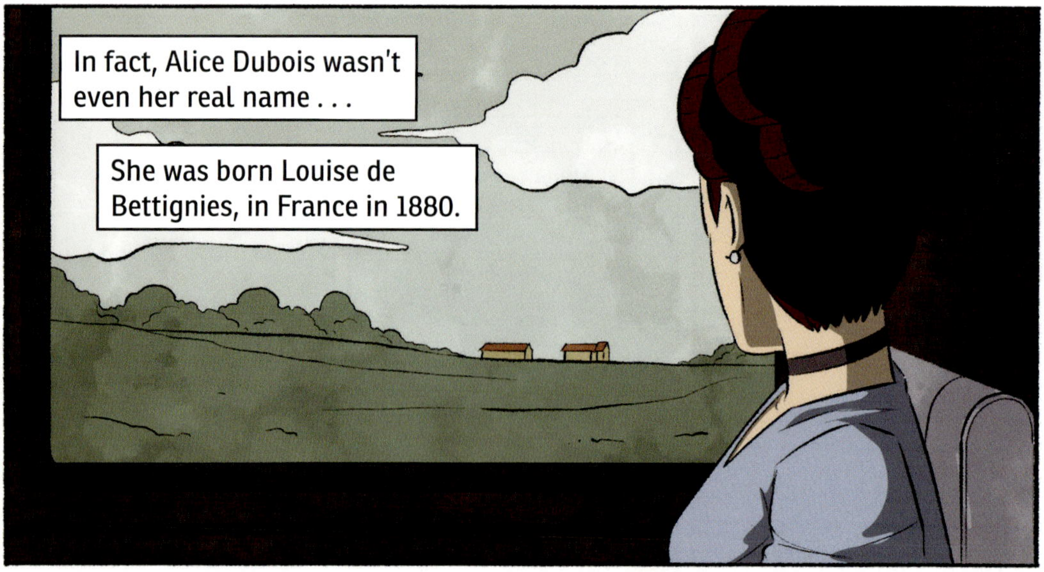
In fact, Alice Dubois wasn't even her real name . . .
She was born Louise de Bettignies, in France in 1880.

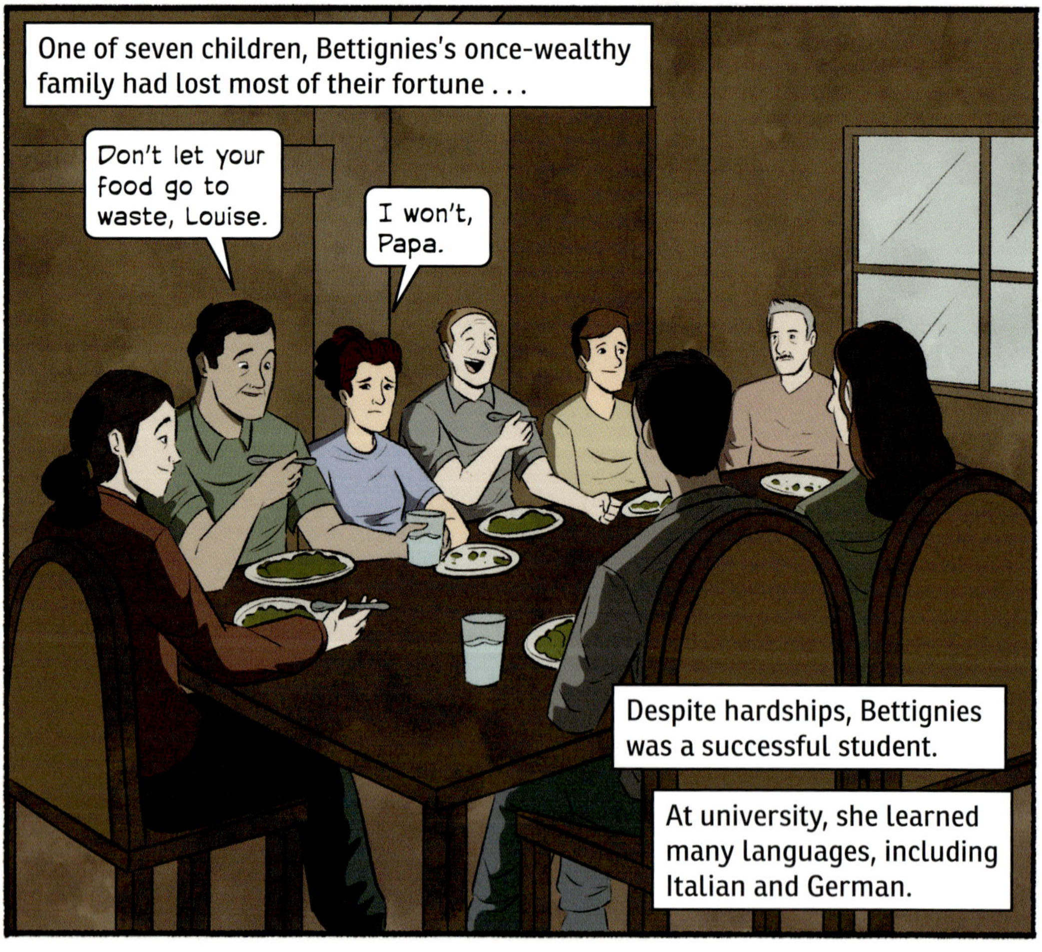
One of seven children, Bettignies's once-wealthy family had lost most of their fortune . . .
Don't let your food go to waste, Louise.
I won't, Papa.
Despite hardships, Bettignies was a successful student.
At university, she learned many languages, including Italian and German.

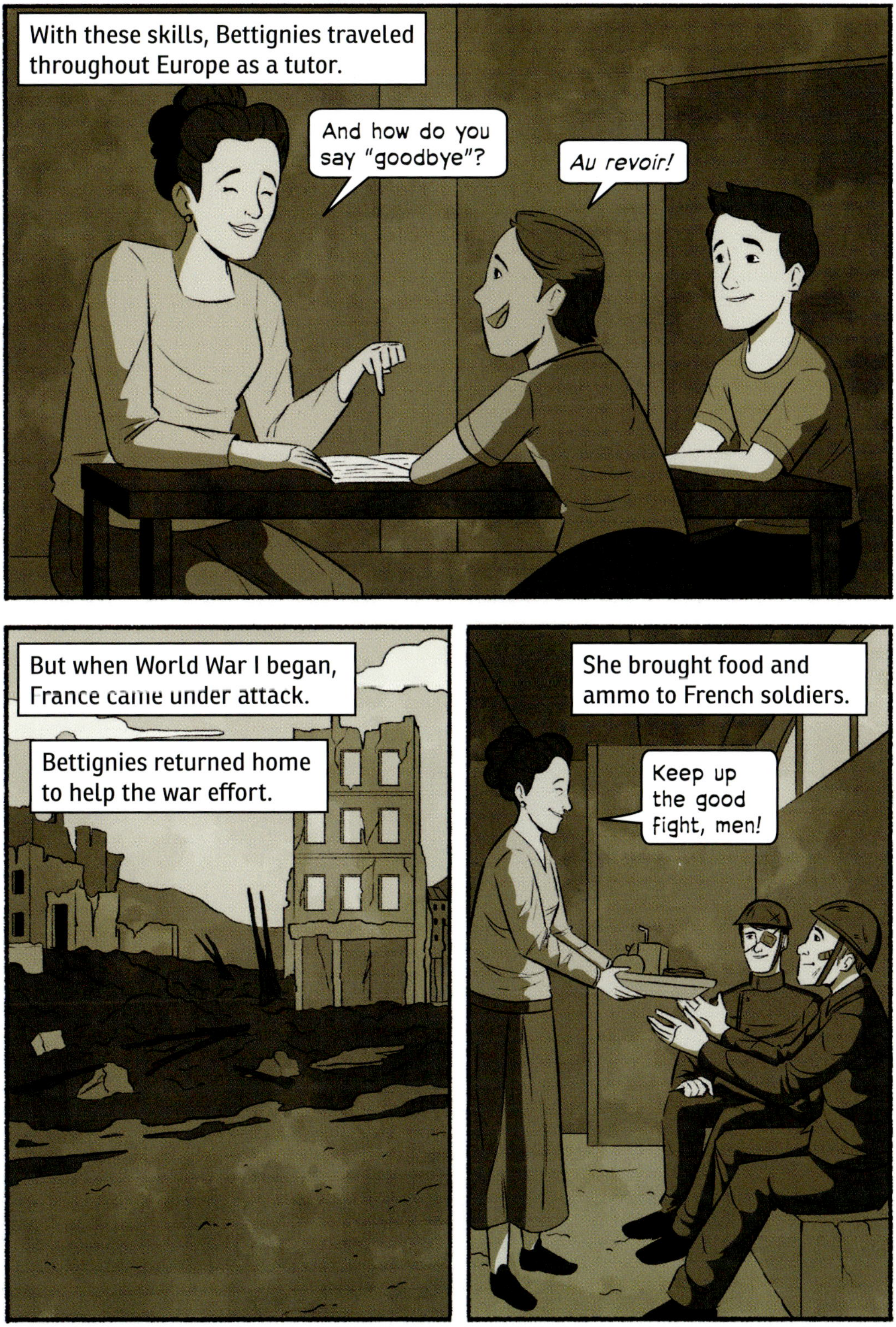

With these skills, Bettignies traveled throughout Europe as a tutor.
And how do you say "goodbye"?
Au revoir!
But when World War I began, France came under attack.
Bettignies returned home to help the war effort.
She brought food and ammo to French soldiers.
Keep up the good fight, men!

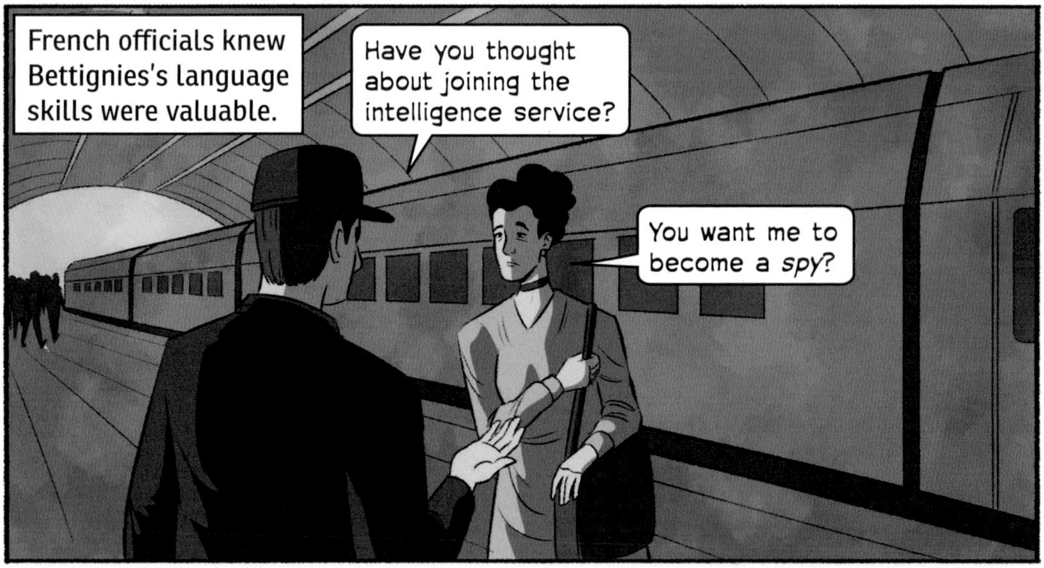
French officials knew Bettignies's language skills were valuable.
Have you thought about joining the intelligence service?
You want me to become a *spy*?

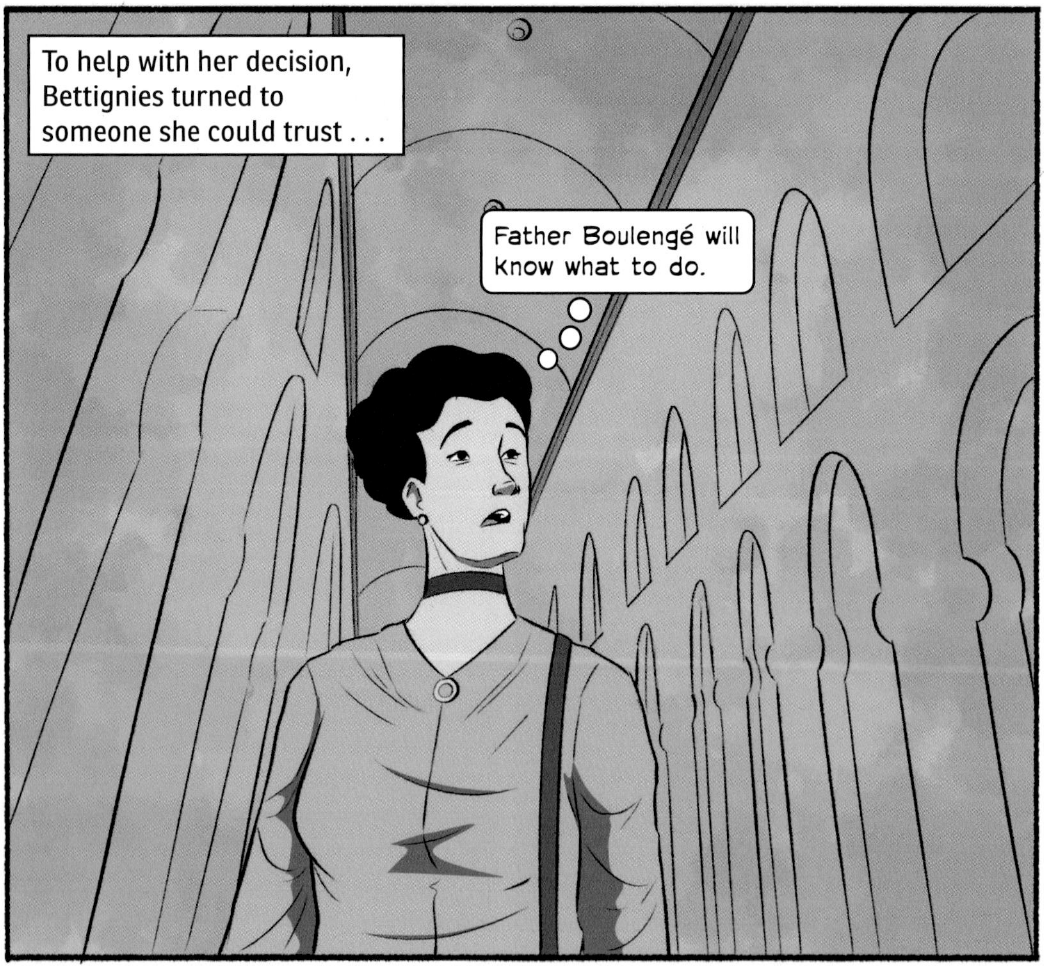
To help with her decision, Bettignies turned to someone she could trust . . .
Father Boulengé will know what to do.

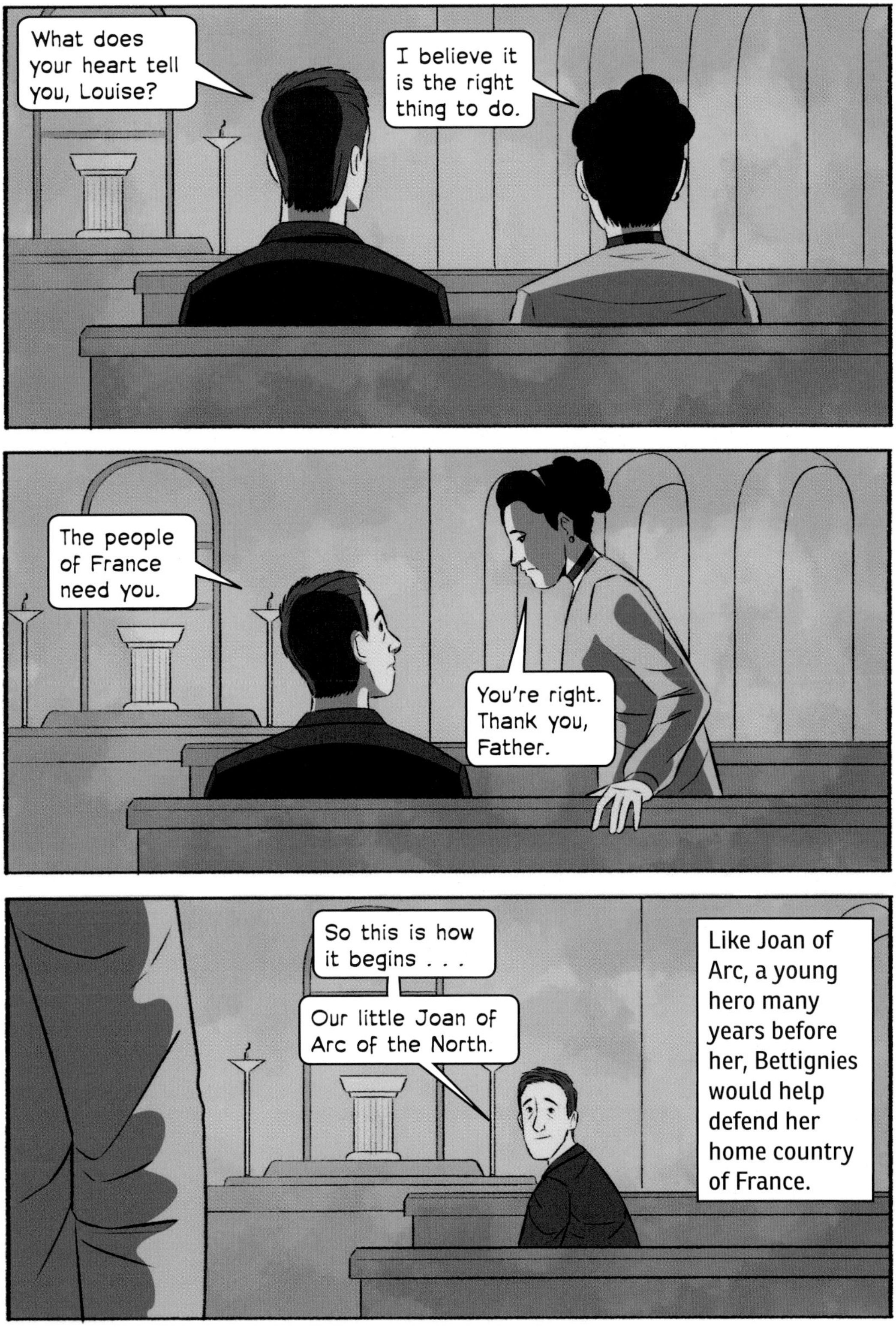

What does your heart tell you, Louise?
I believe it is the right thing to do.
The people of France need you.
You're right. Thank you, Father.
So this is how it begins . . .
Our little Joan of Arc of the North.
Like Joan of Arc, a young hero many years before her, Bettignies would help defend her home country of France.

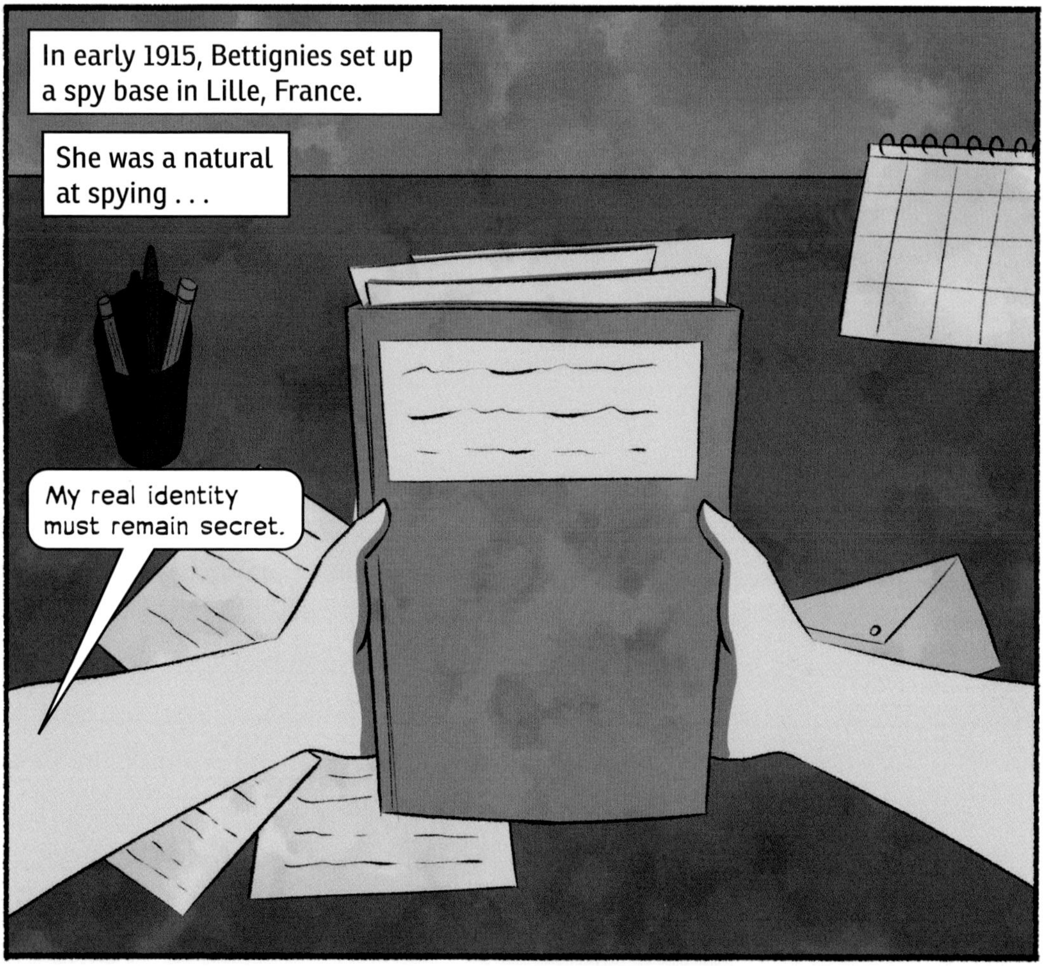
In early 1915, Bettignies set up a spy base in Lille, France.
She was a natural at spying . . .
My real identity must remain secret.

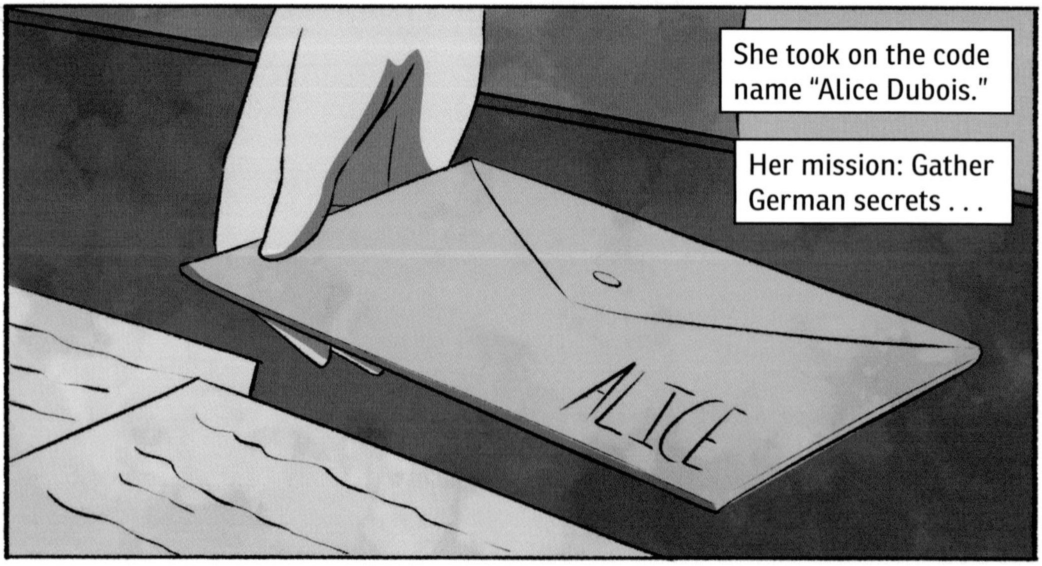
She took on the code name "Alice Dubois."
Her mission: Gather German secrets . . .
ALICE

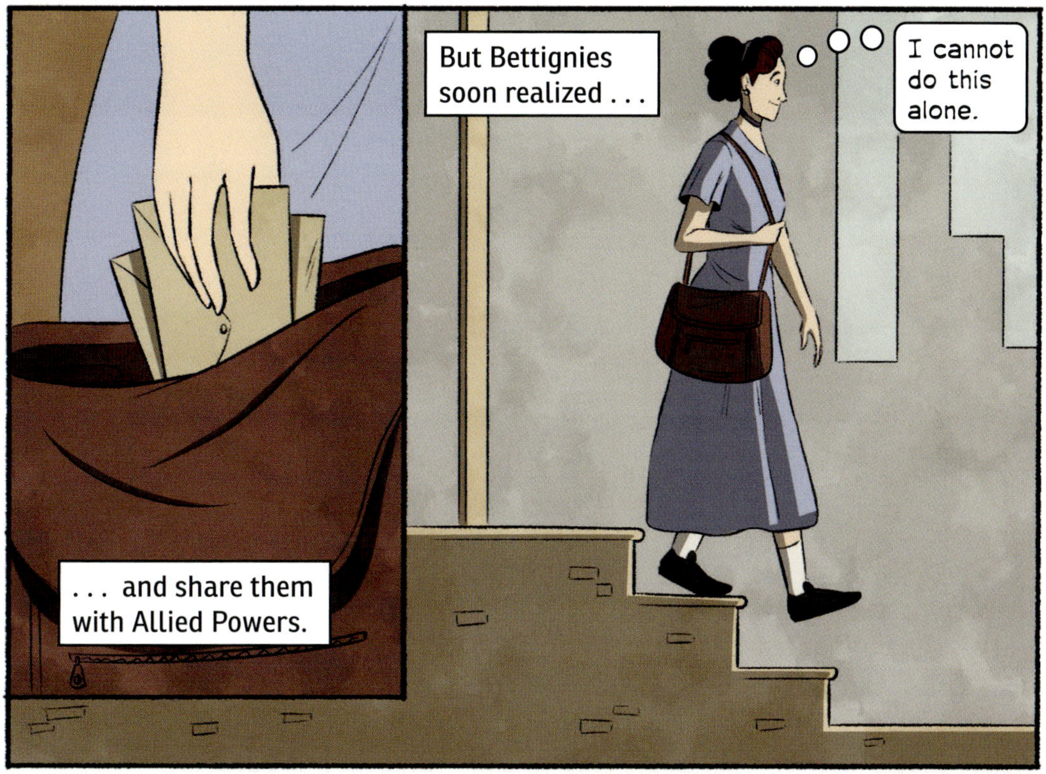
. . . and share them with Allied Powers.
But Bettignies soon realized . . .
I cannot do this alone.

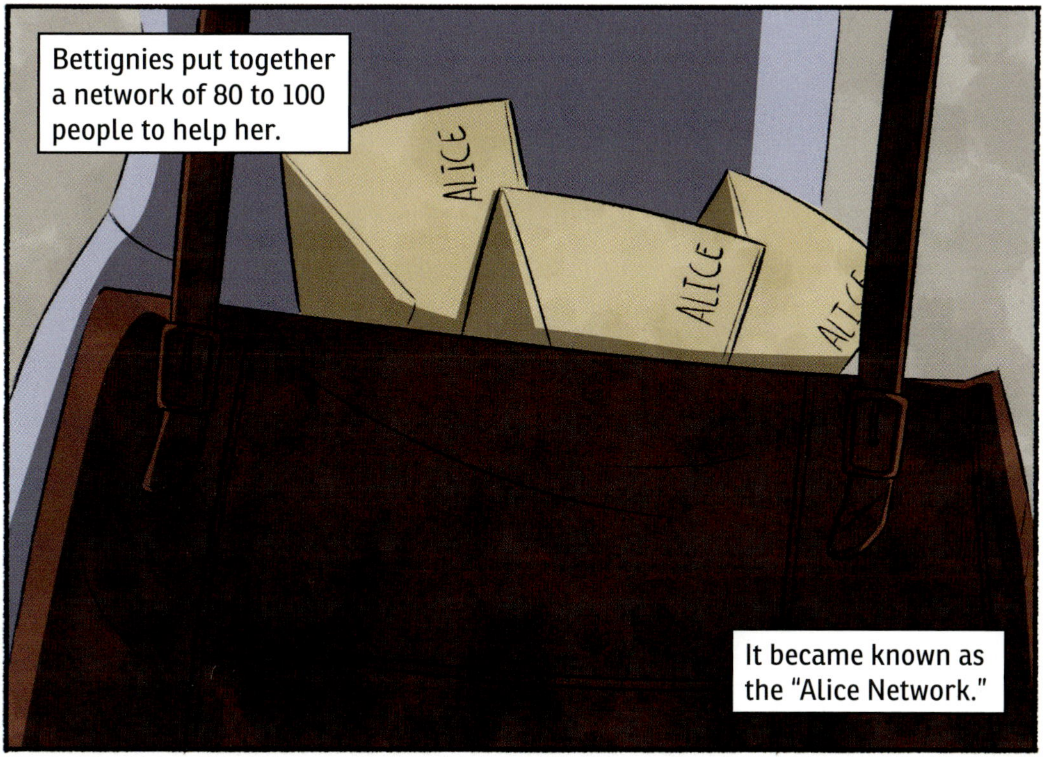
Bettignies put together a network of 80 to 100 people to help her.
ALICE
ALICE
It became known as the "Alice Network."

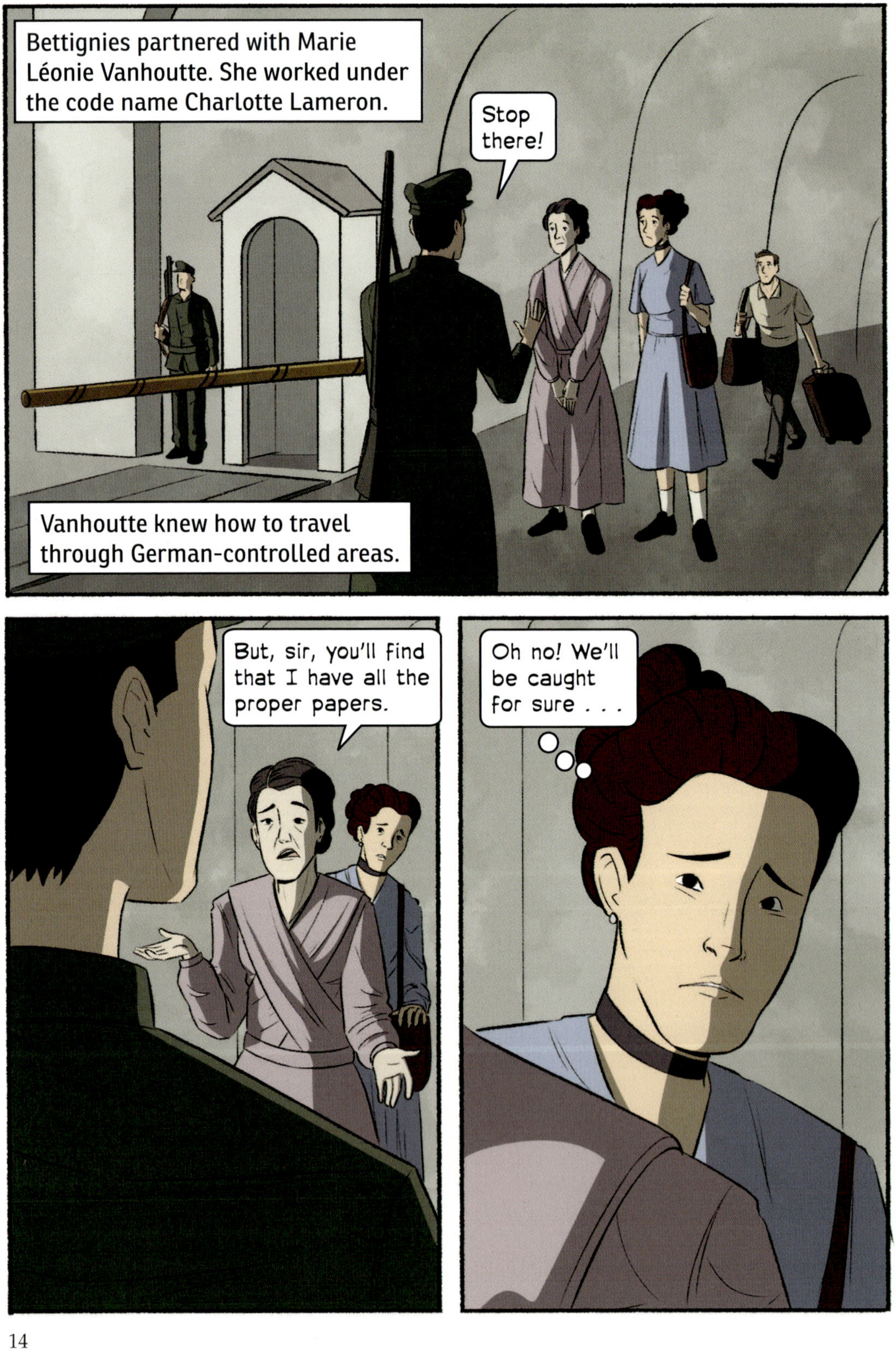
Bettignies partnered with Marie Léonie Vanhoutte. She worked under the code name Charlotte Lameron.
Stop there!
Vanhoutte knew how to travel through German-controlled areas.
But, sir, you'll find that I have all the proper papers.
Oh no! We'll be caught for sure . . .

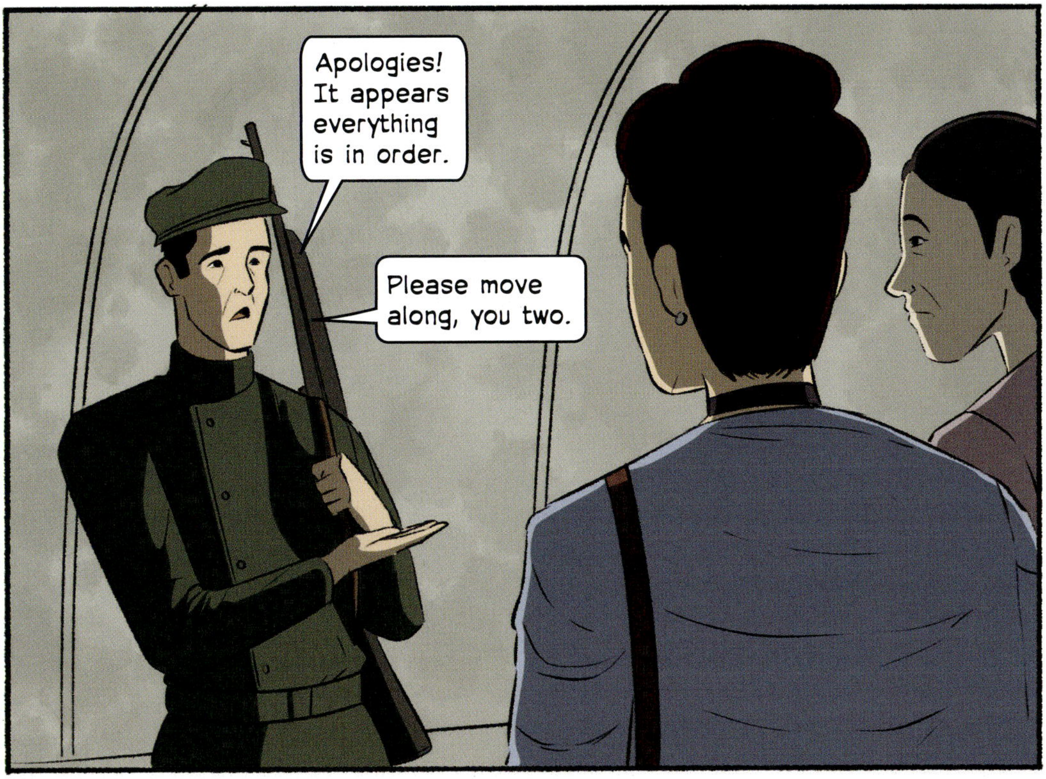
Apologies! It appears everything is in order.
Please move along, you two.

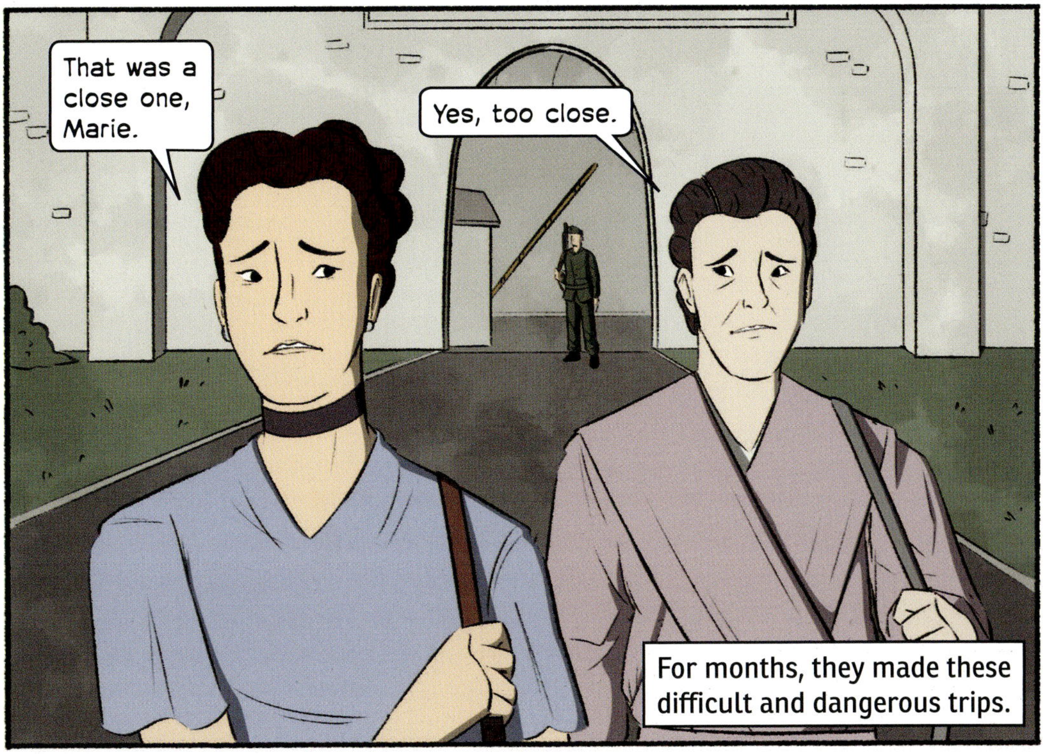
That was a close one, Marie.
Yes, too close.
For months, they made these difficult and dangerous trips.

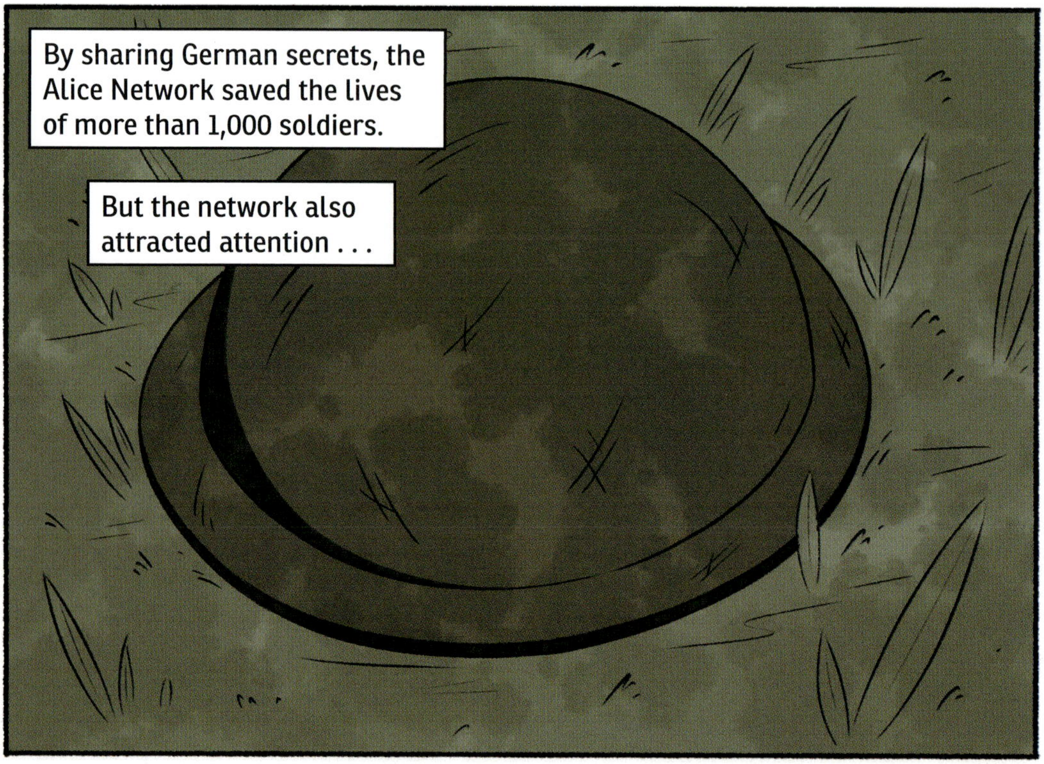
By sharing German secrets, the Alice Network saved the lives of more than 1,000 soldiers.
But the network also attracted attention . . .

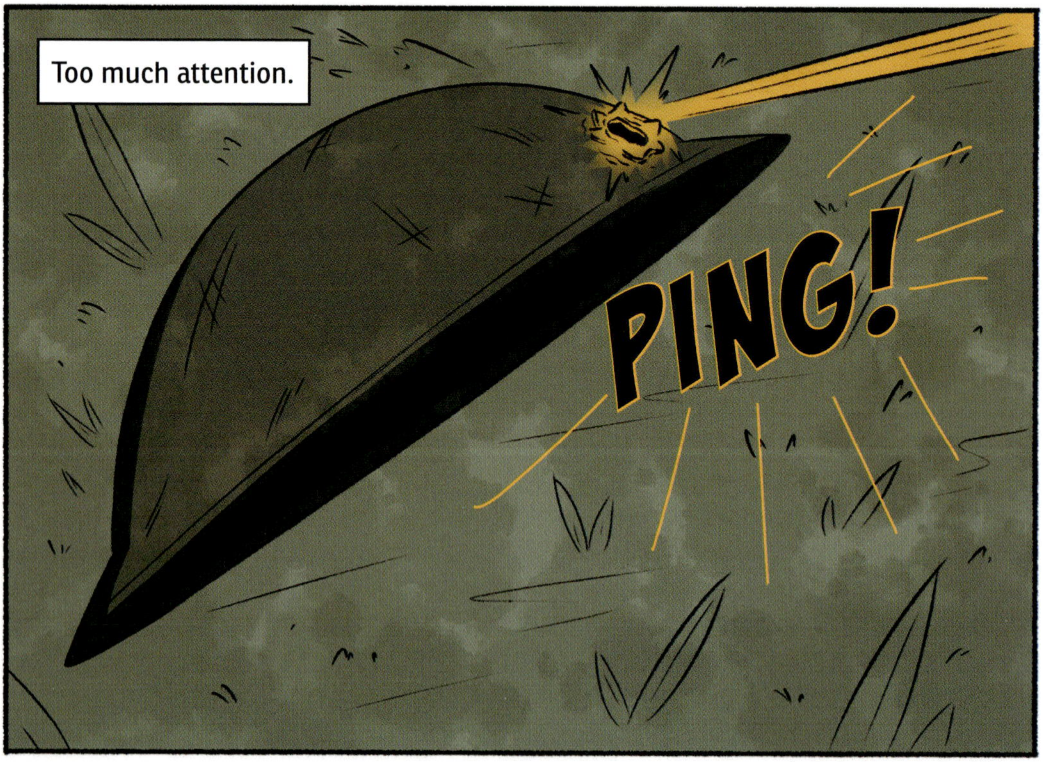
Too much attention.
PING!

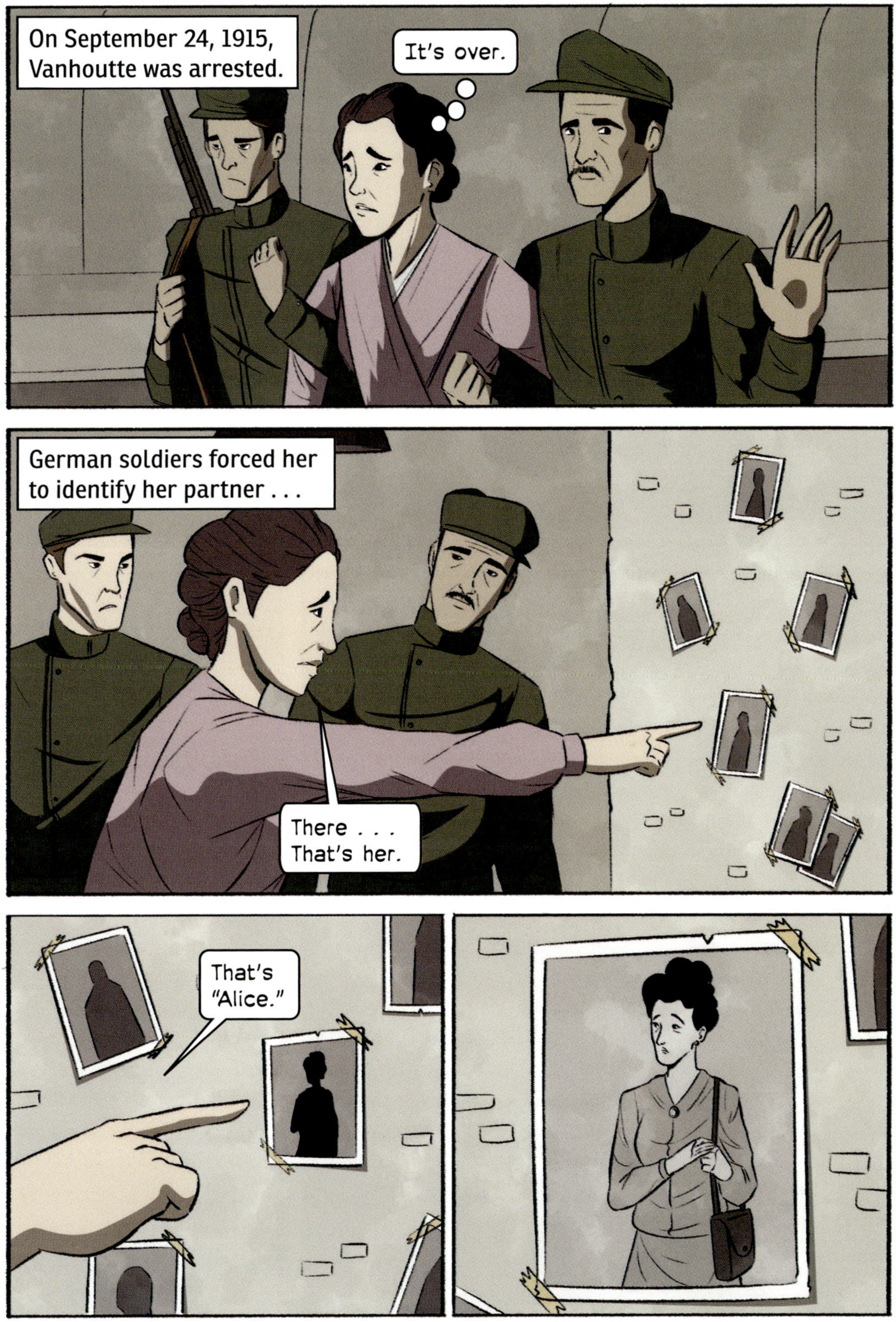
On September 24, 1915, Vanhoutte was arrested.
It's over.
German soldiers forced her to identify her partner . . .
There . . . That's her.
That's "Alice."

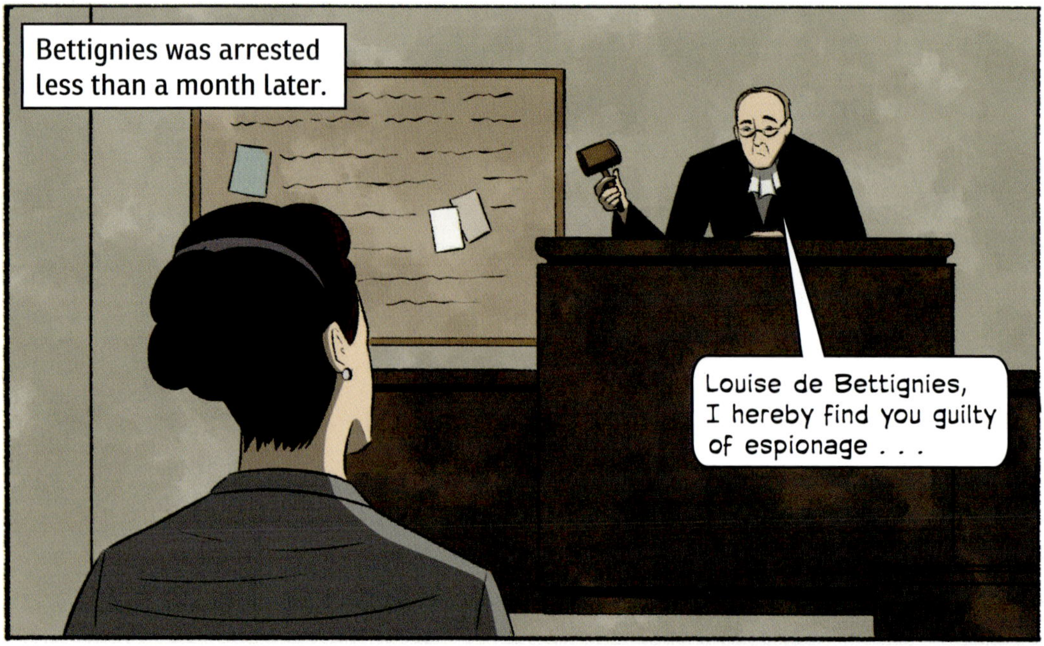
Bettignies was arrested less than a month later.
Louise de Bettignies, I hereby find you guilty of espionage . . .

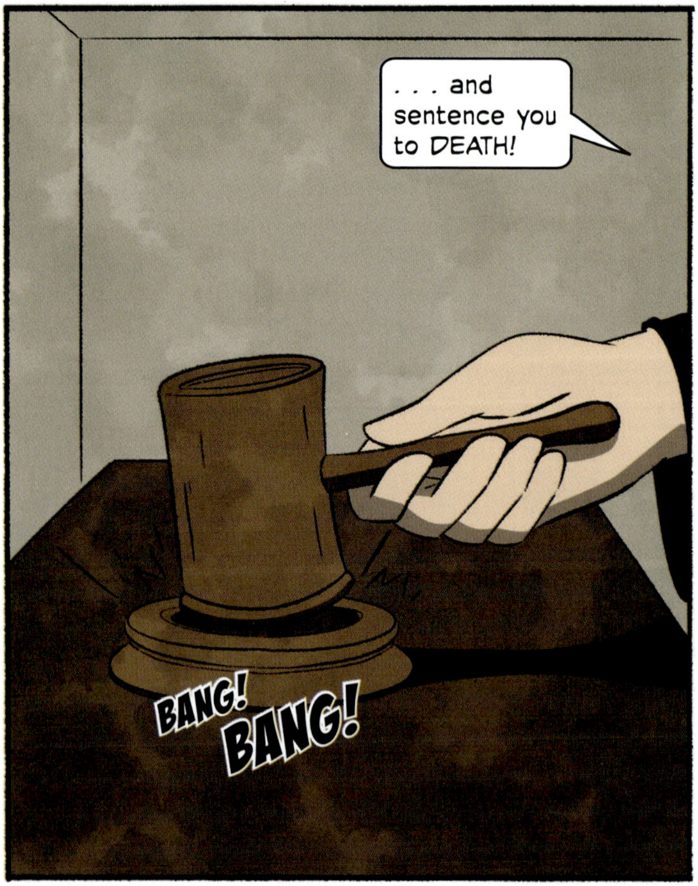
. . . and sentence you to DEATH!
BANG!
BANG!

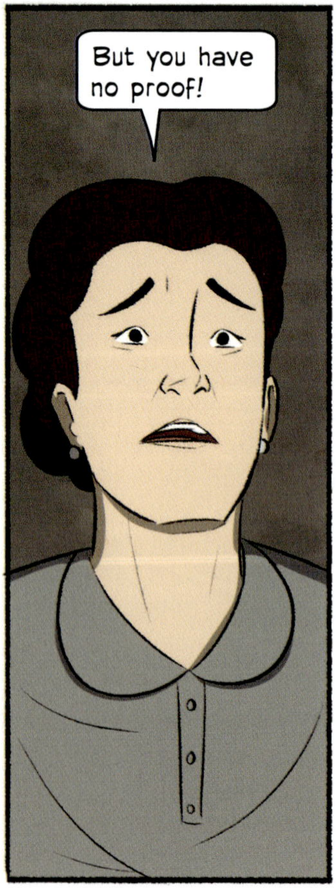
But you have no proof!

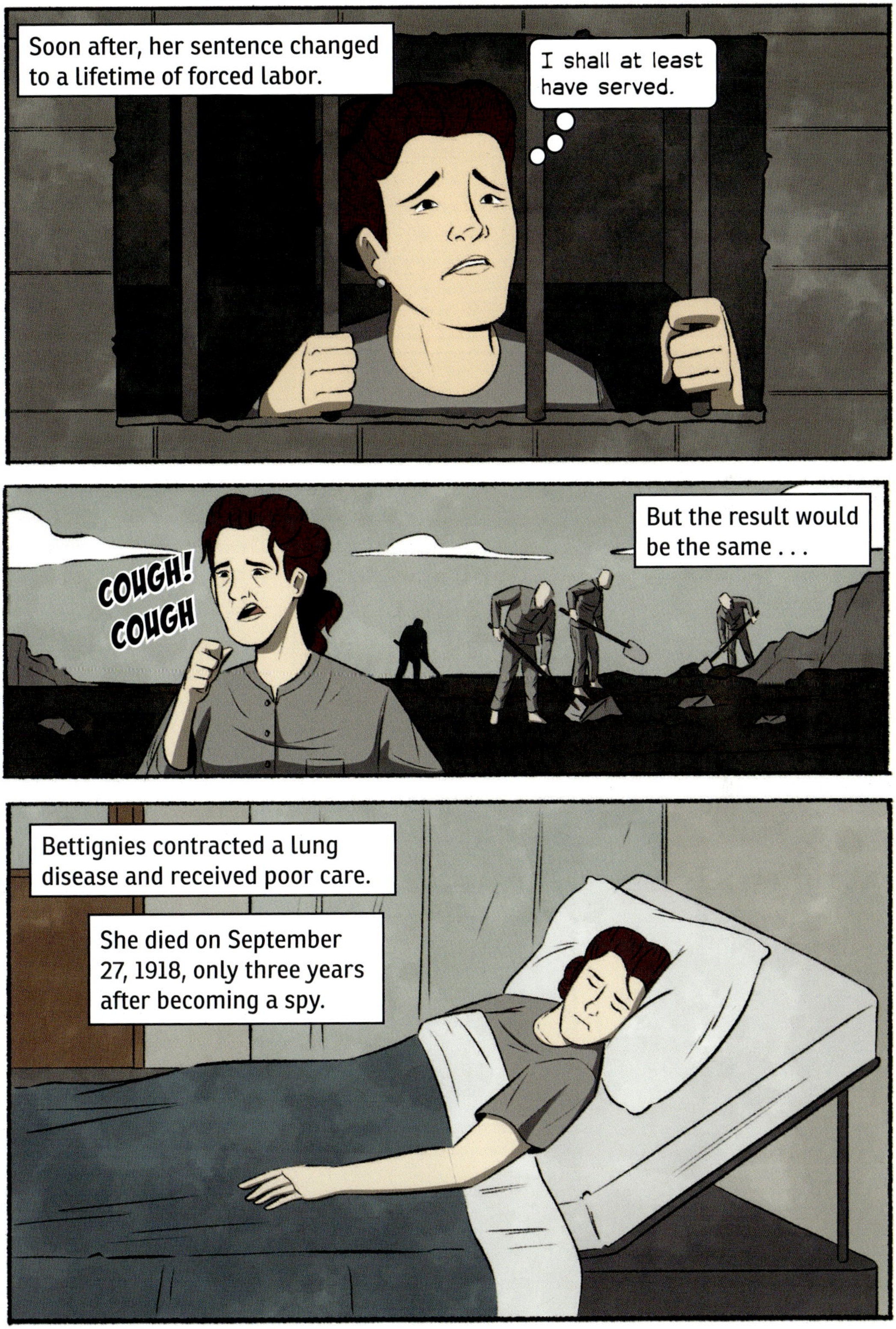
Soon after, her sentence changed to a lifetime of forced labor.
I shall at least have served.
COUGH! COUGH
But the result would be the same . . .
Bettignies contracted a lung disease and received poor care.
She died on September 27, 1918, only three years after becoming a spy.

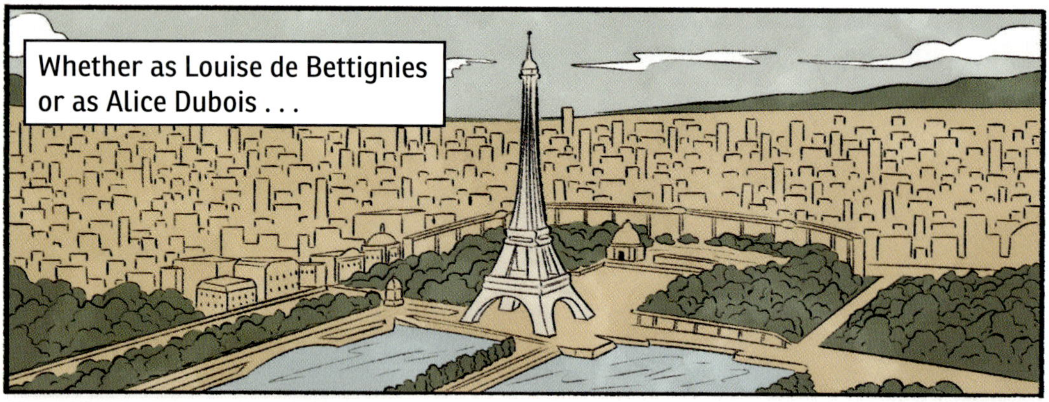
Whether as Louise de Bettignies or as Alice Dubois . . .

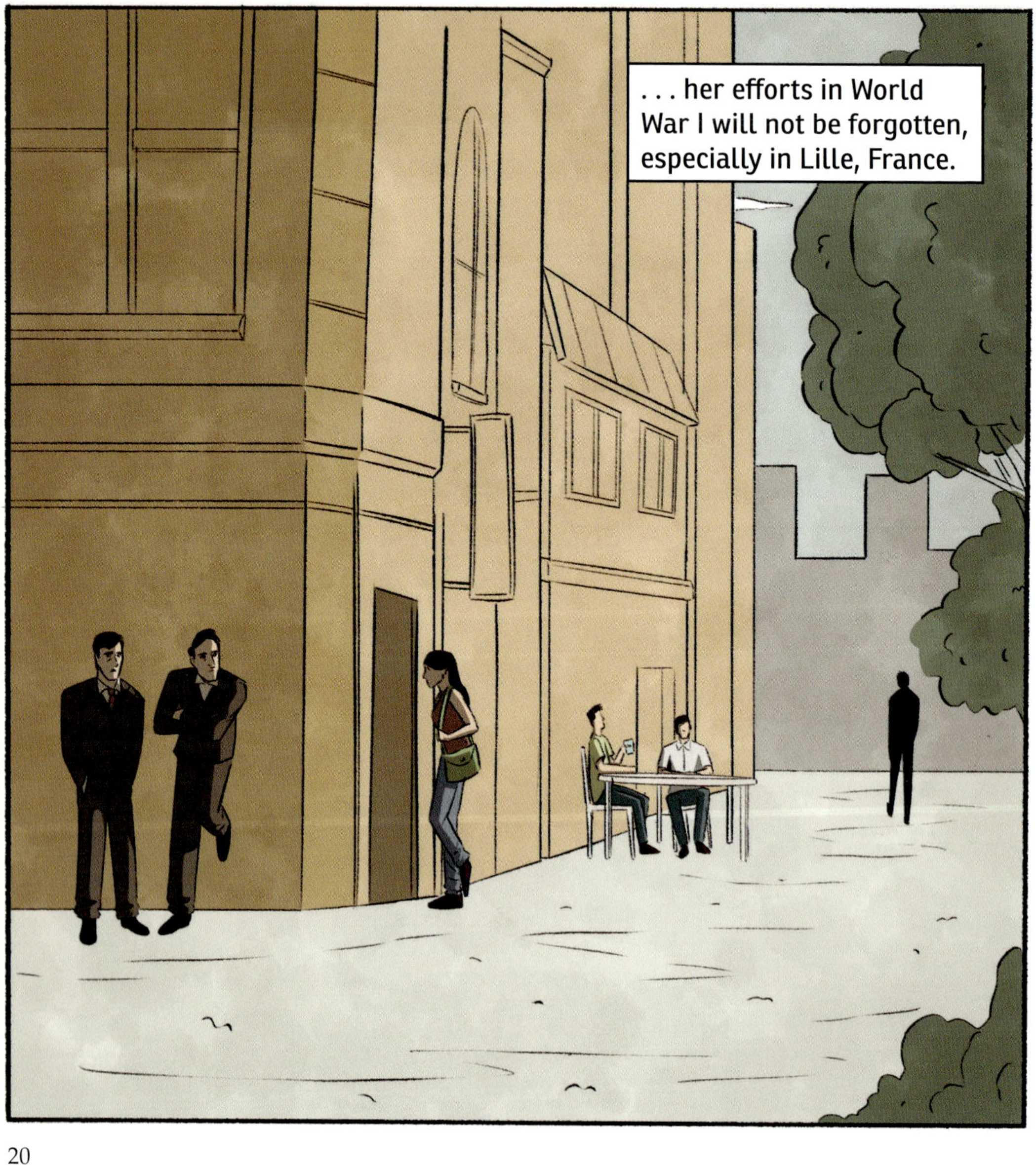
. . . her efforts in World War I will not be forgotten, especially in Lille, France.

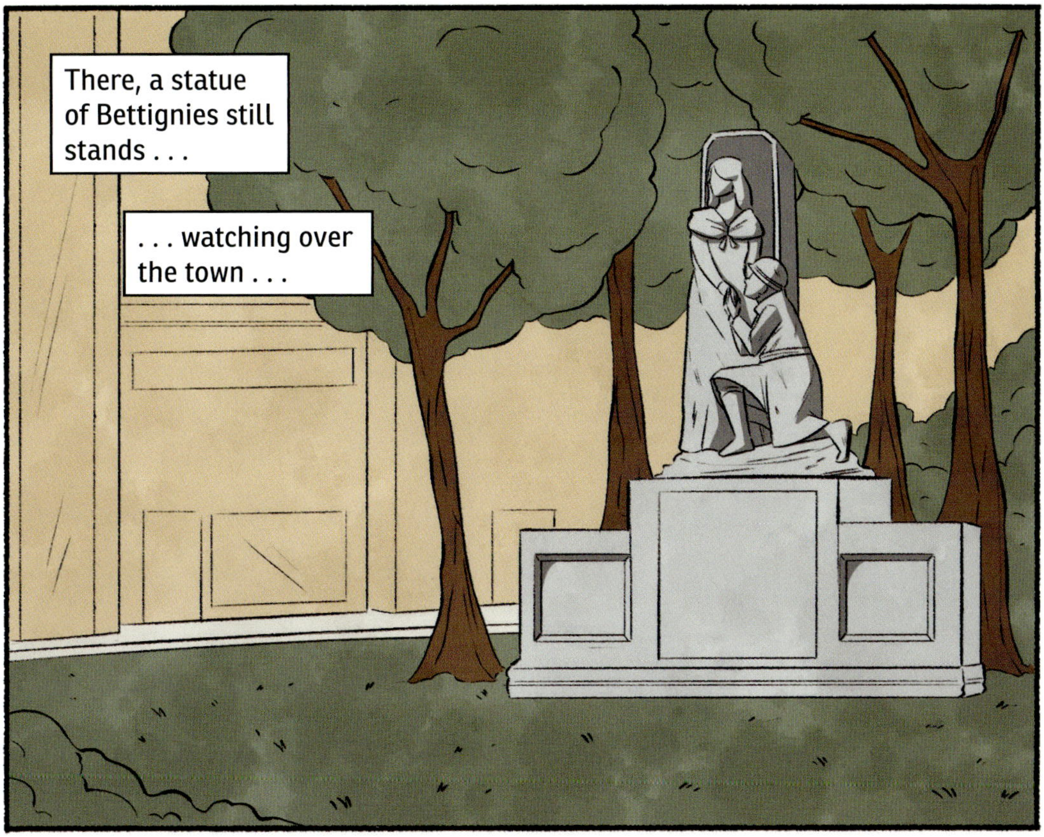
There, a statue of Bettignies still stands . . .
. . . watching over the town . . .

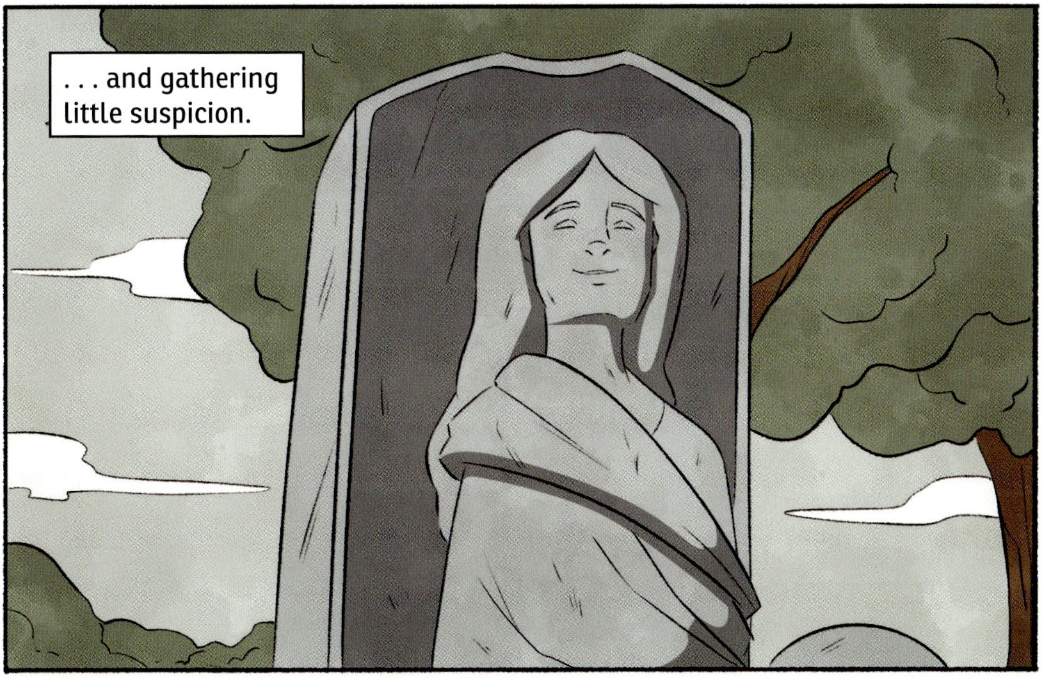
. . . and gathering little suspicion.

CHAPTER TWO

RICHARD B. TINSLEY: SPY TO A "T"

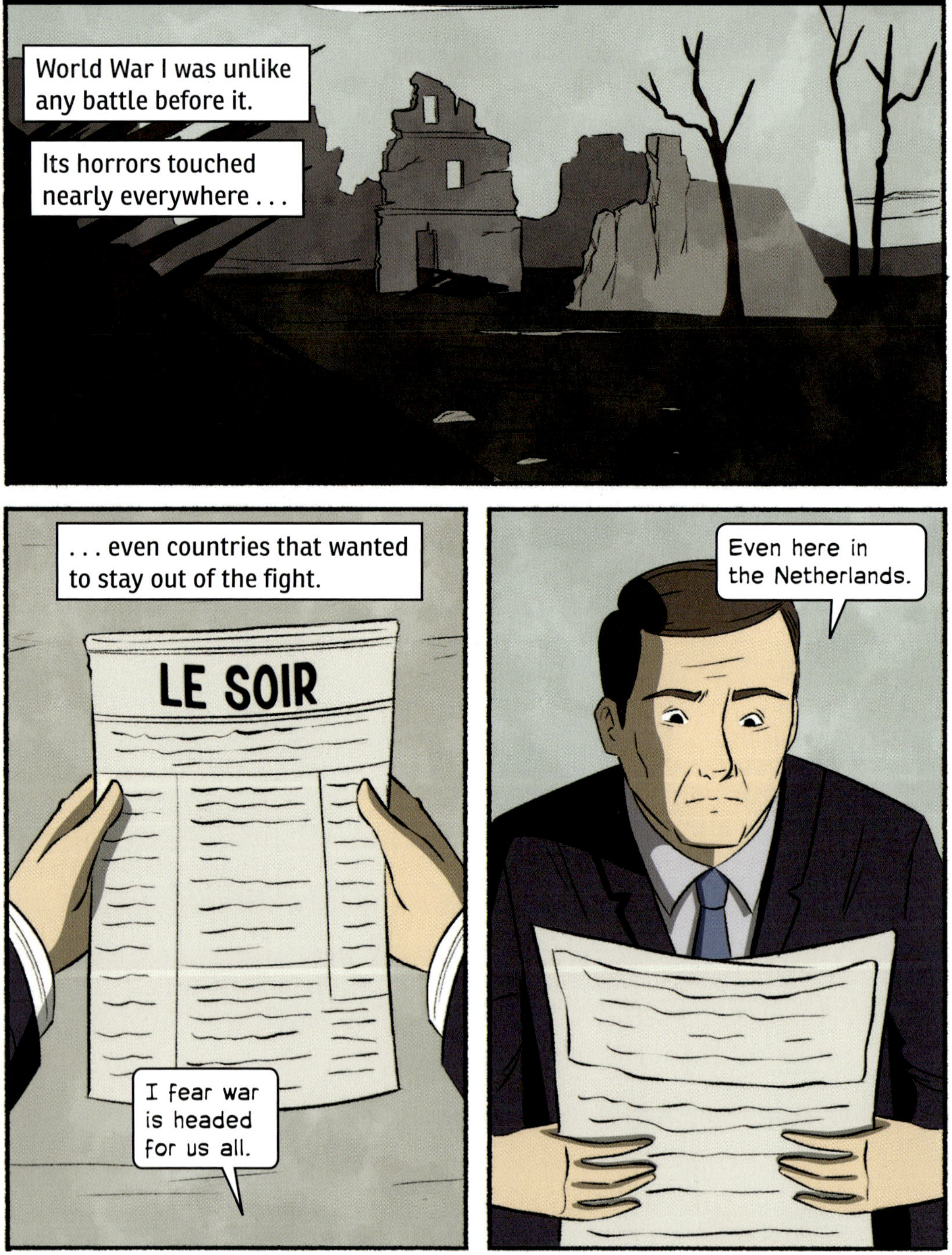
World War I was unlike any battle before it.
Its horrors touched nearly everywhere . . .
. . . even countries that wanted to stay out of the fight.
LE SOIR
I fear war is headed for us all.
Even here in the Netherlands.

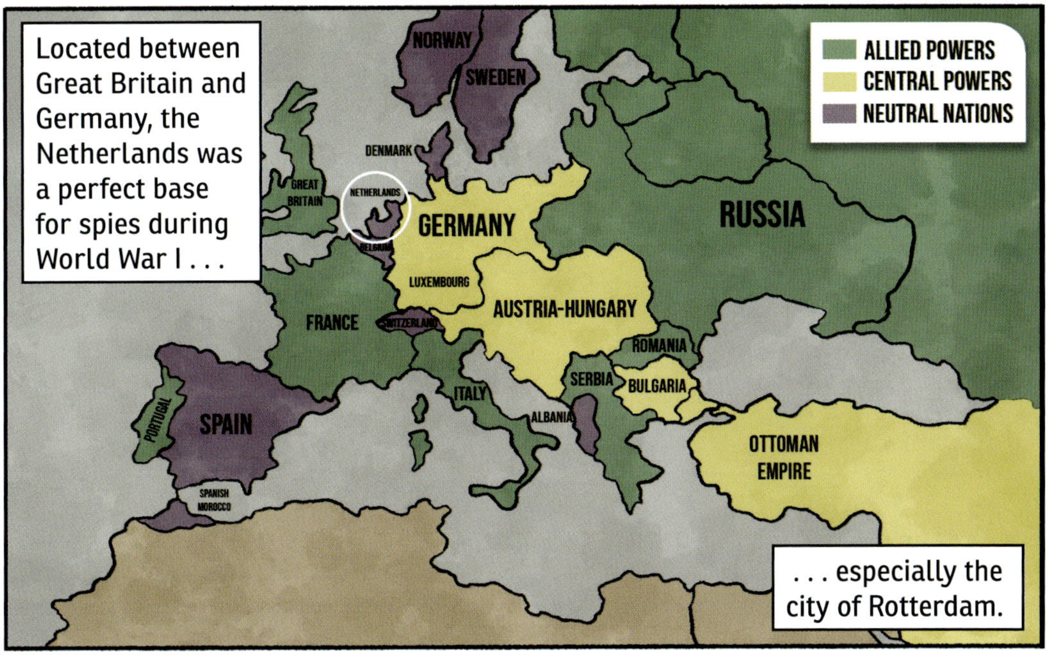
Located between Great Britain and Germany, the Netherlands was a perfect base for spies during World War I . . .
ALLIED POWERS
CENTRAL POWERS
NEUTRAL NATIONS
NORWAY
SWEDEN
DENMARK
GREAT BRITAIN
NETHERLANDS
BELGIUM
GERMANY
RUSSIA
LUXEMBOURG
FRANCE
SWITZERLAND
AUSTRIA-HUNGARY
ROMANIA
SERBIA
BULGARIA
ITALY
ALBANIA
PORTUGAL
SPAIN
SPANISH MOROCCO
OTTOMAN EMPIRE
. . . especially the city of Rotterdam.

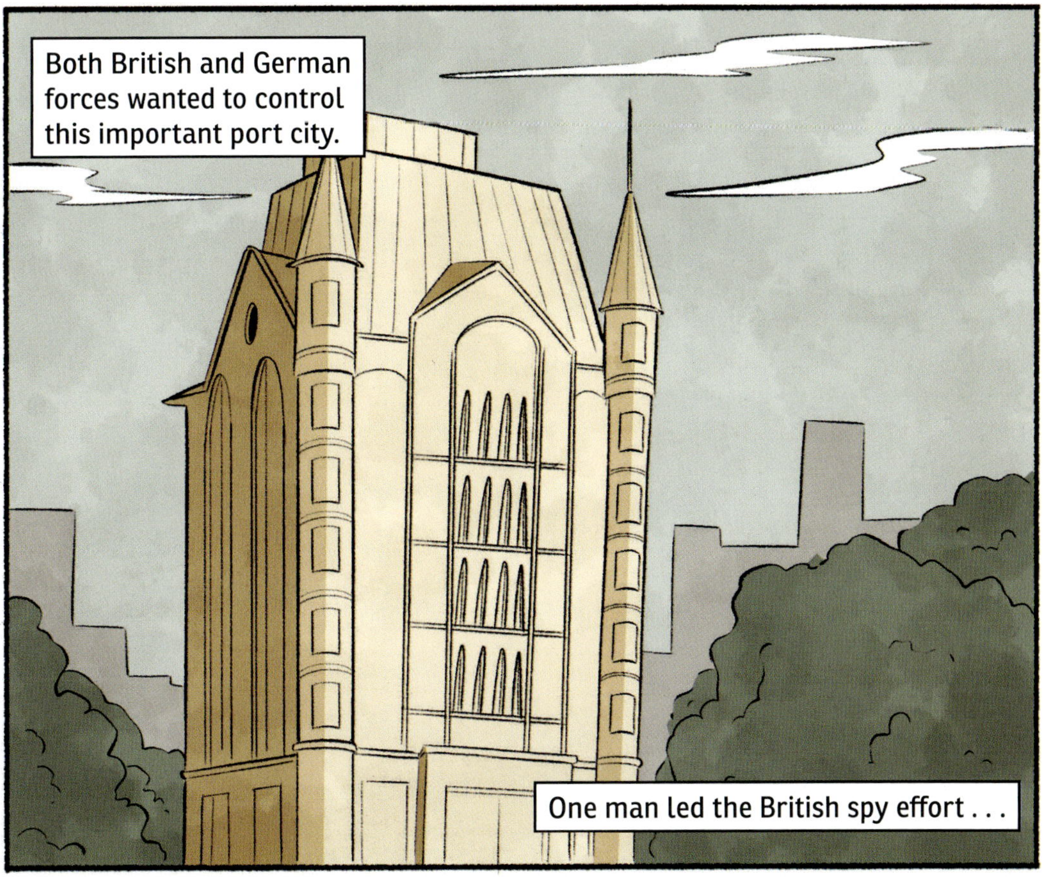
Both British and German forces wanted to control this important port city.
One man led the British spy effort . . .

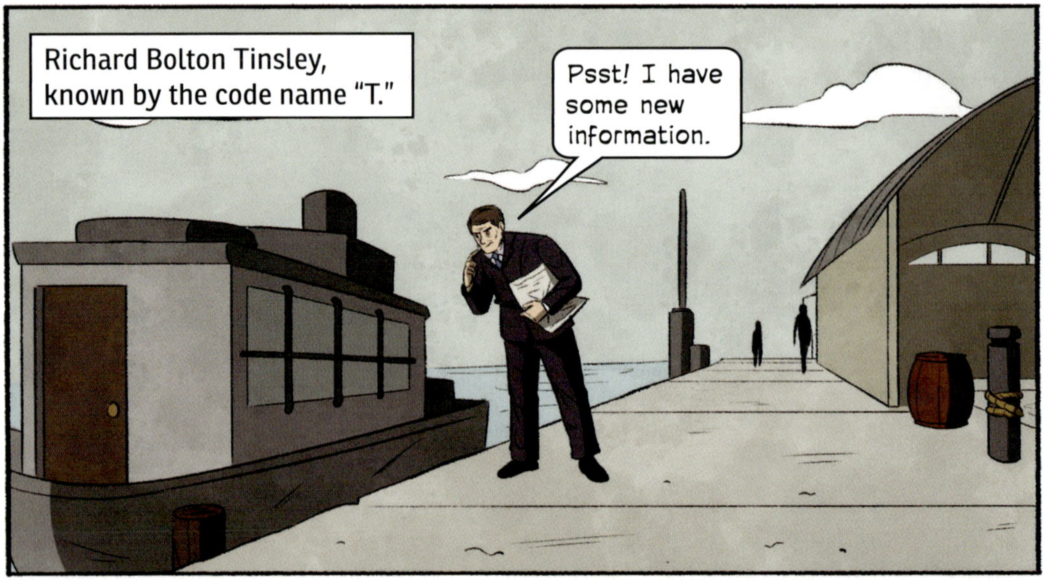
Richard Bolton Tinsley, known by the code name "T."
Psst! I have some new information.

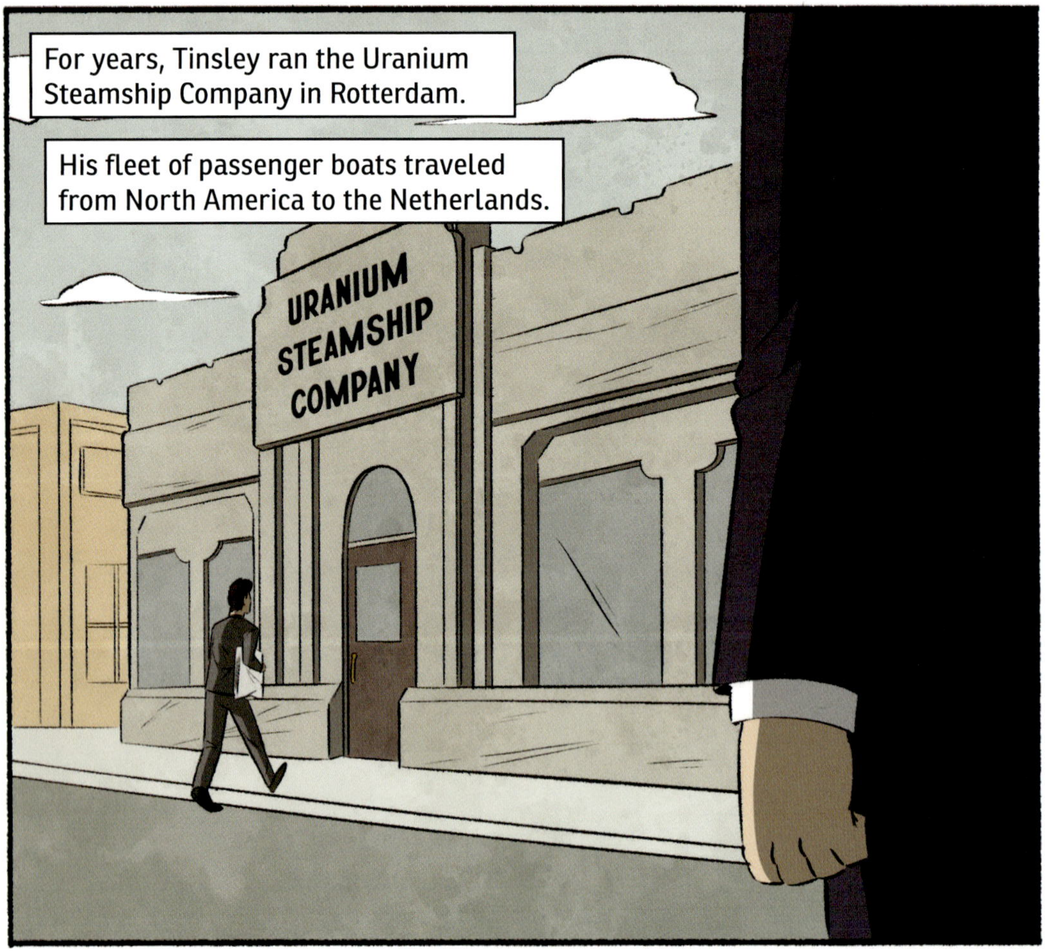
For years, Tinsley ran the Uranium Steamship Company in Rotterdam.
His fleet of passenger boats traveled from North America to the Netherlands.
URANIUM STEAMSHIP COMPANY

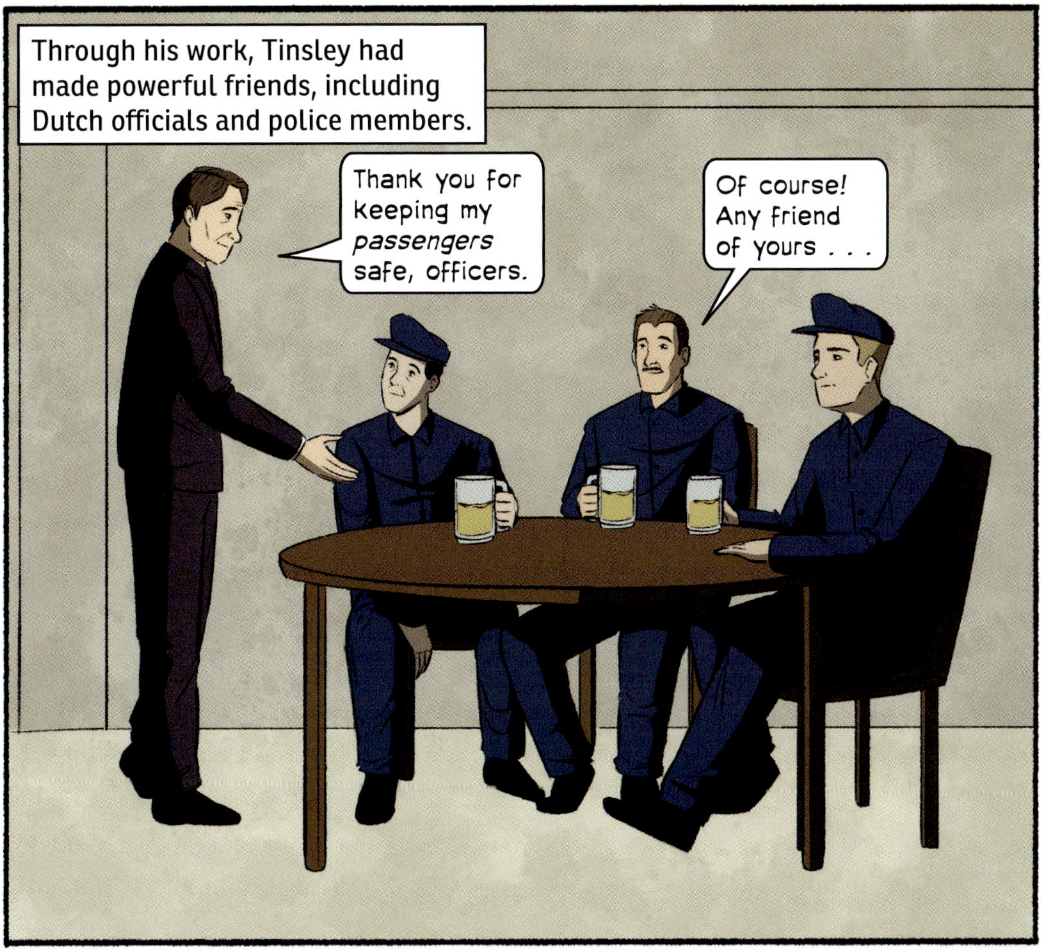
Through his work, Tinsley had made powerful friends, including Dutch officials and police members.
Thank you for keeping my *passengers* safe, officers.
Of course! Any friend of yours . . .

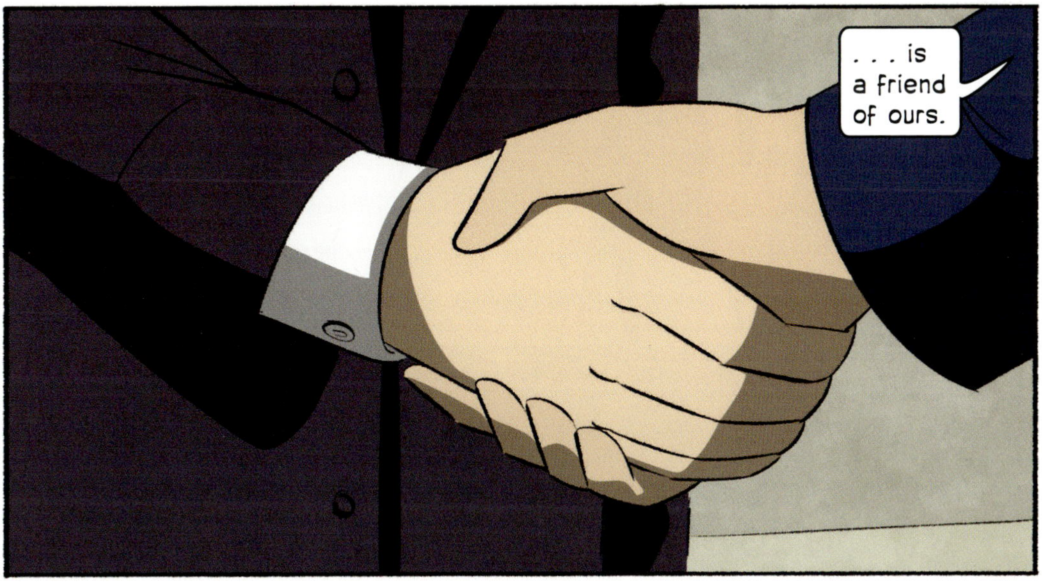
. . . is a friend of ours.

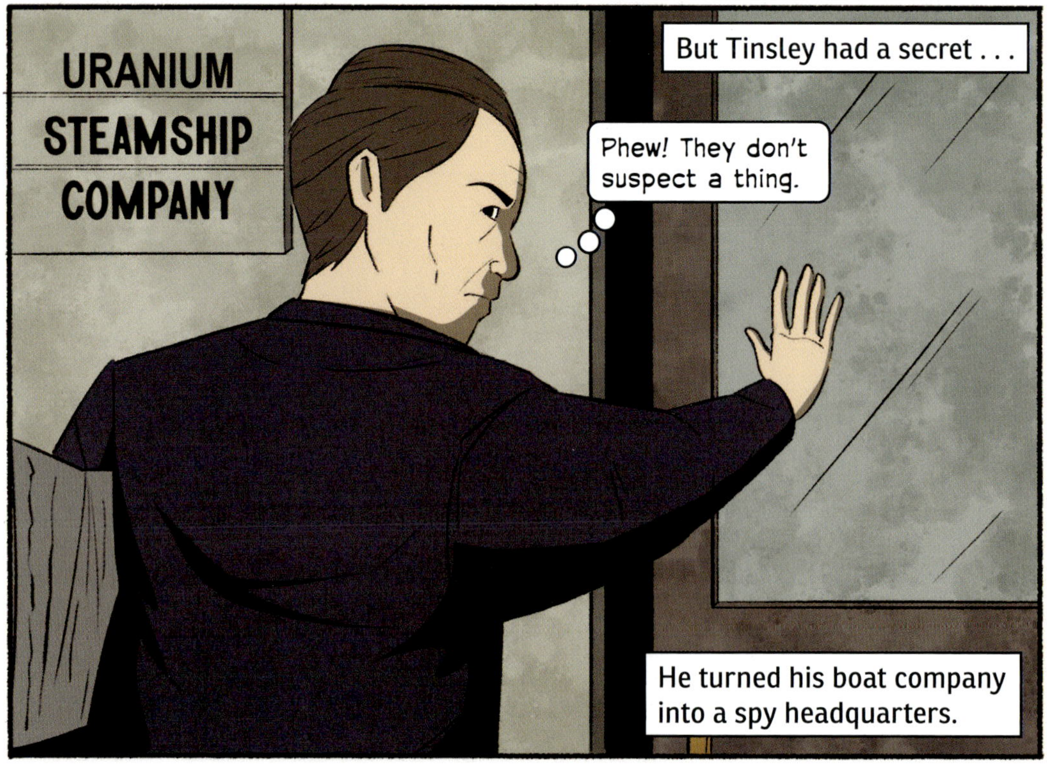
URANIUM
STEAMSHIP
COMPANY
But Tinsley had a secret . . .
Phew! They don't suspect a thing.
He turned his boat company into a spy headquarters.

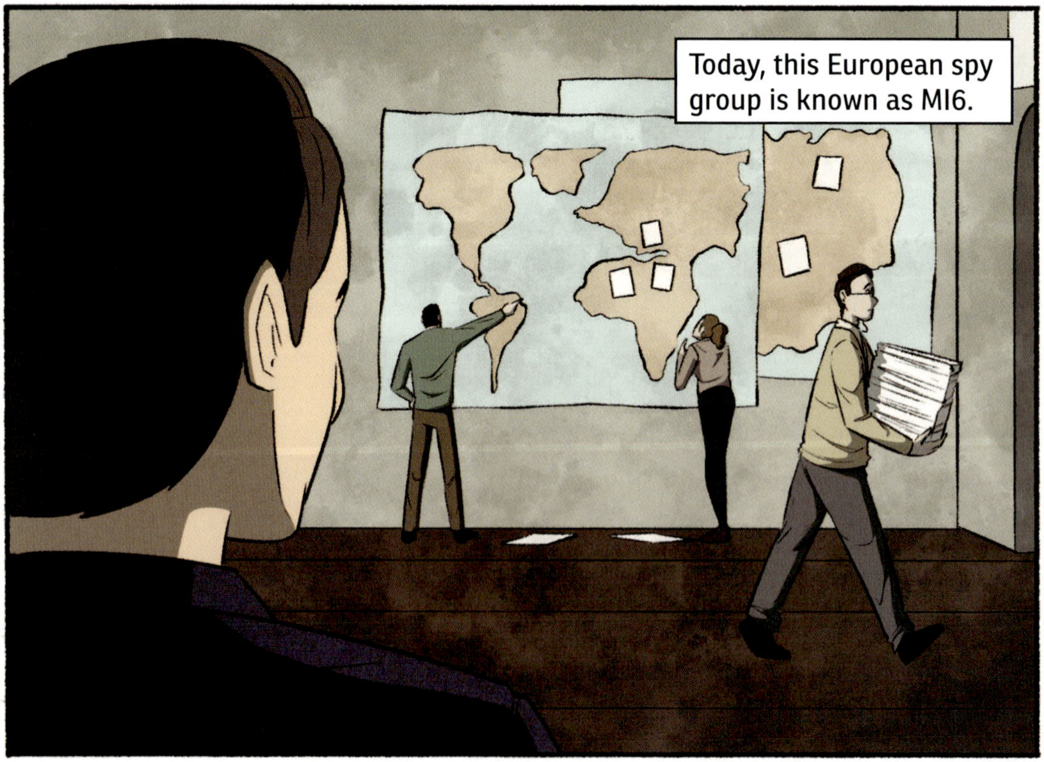
Today, this European spy group is known as MI6.

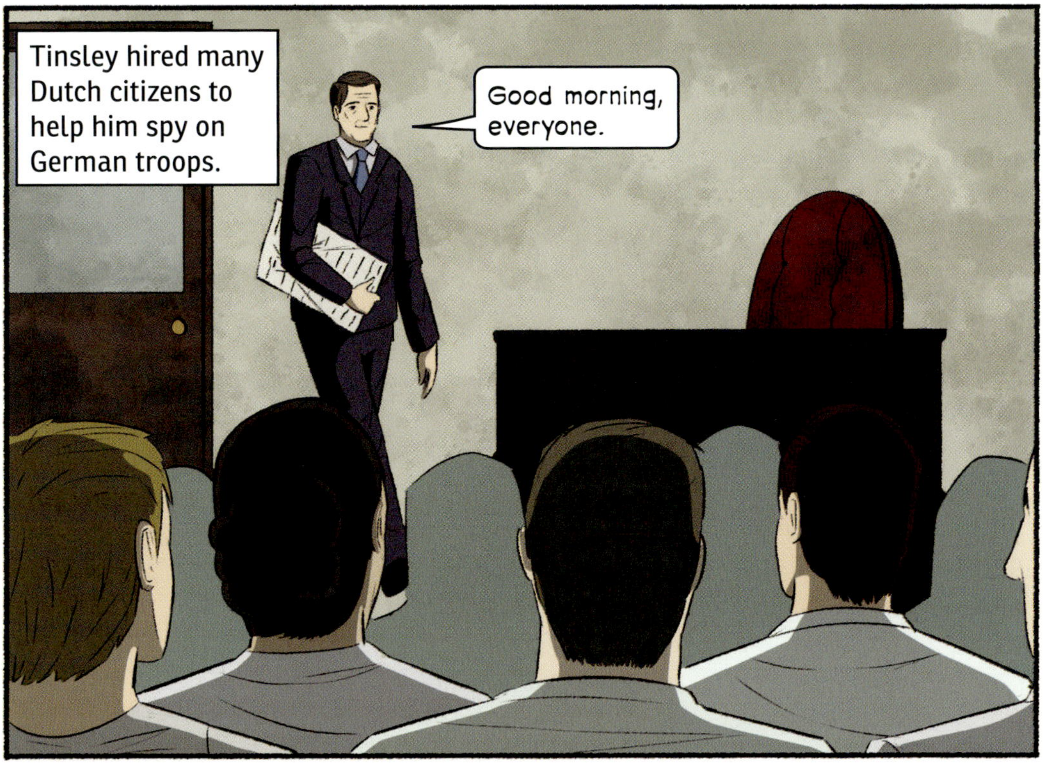
Tinsley hired many Dutch citizens to help him spy on German troops.
Good morning, everyone.

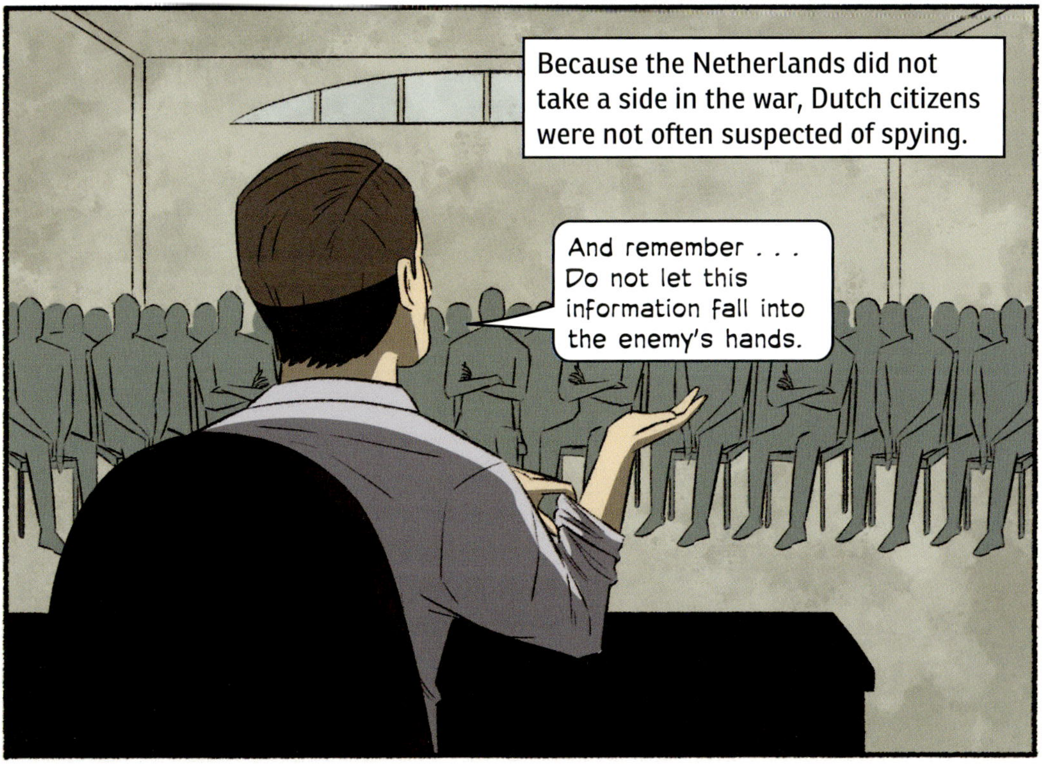
Because the Netherlands did not take a side in the war, Dutch citizens were not often suspected of spying.
And remember . . . Do not let this information fall into the enemy's hands.

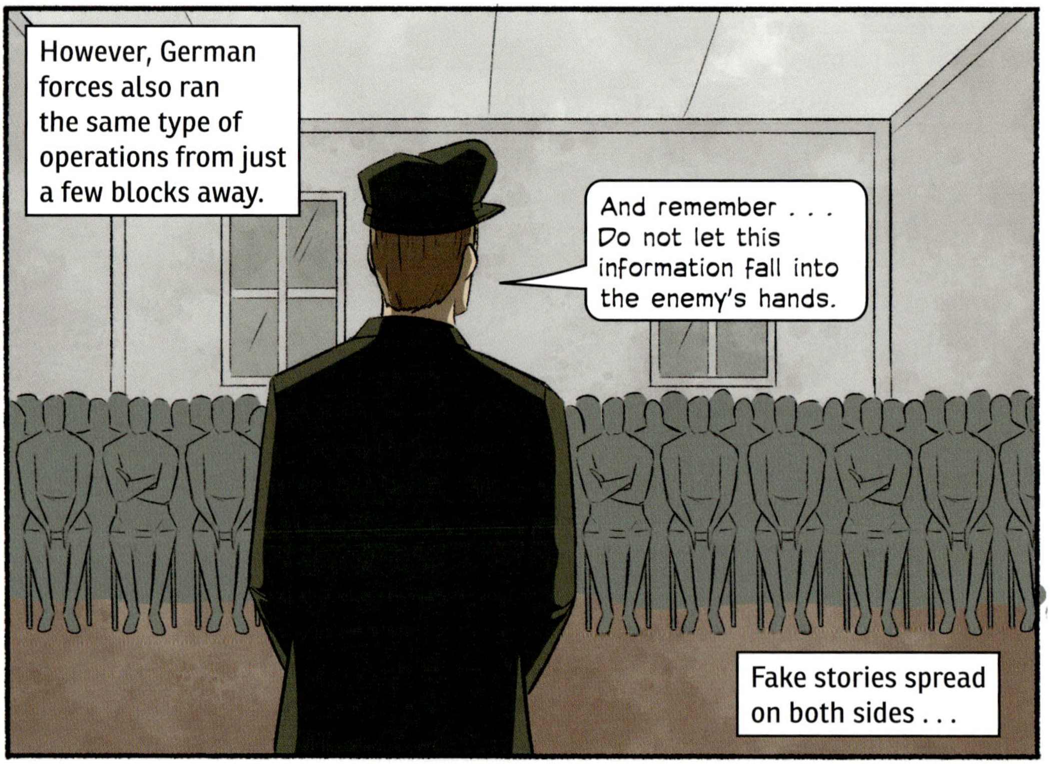
However, German forces also ran the same type of operations from just a few blocks away.
And remember . . . Do not let this information fall into the enemy's hands.
Fake stories spread on both sides . . .

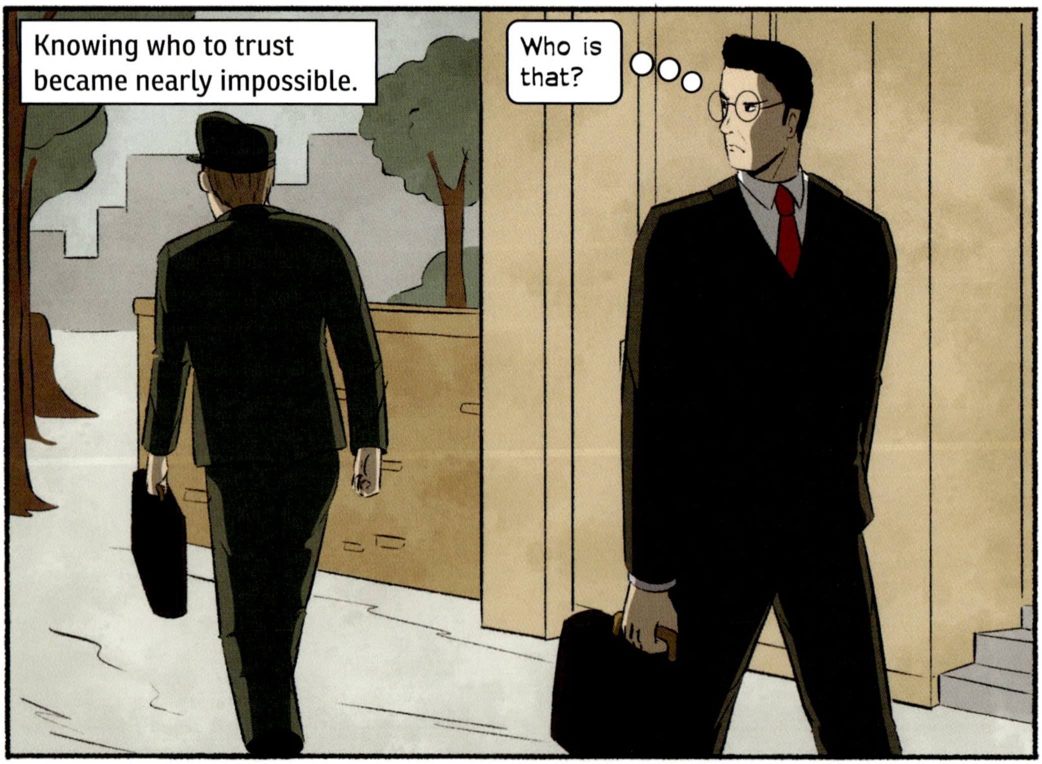
Knowing who to trust became nearly impossible.
Who is that?

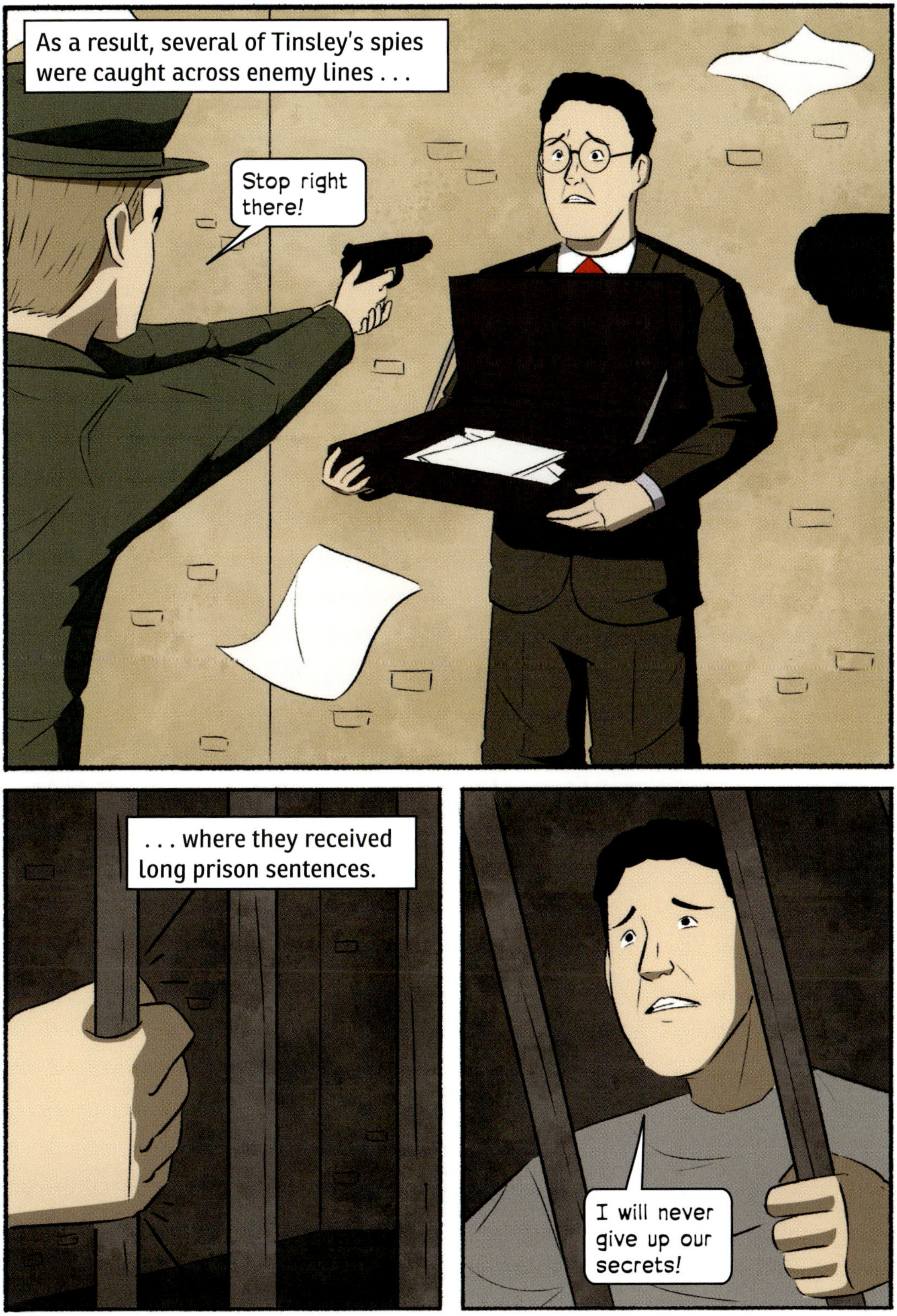
As a result, several of Tinsley's spies were caught across enemy lines . . .
Stop right there!
. . . where they received long prison sentences.
I will never give up our secrets!

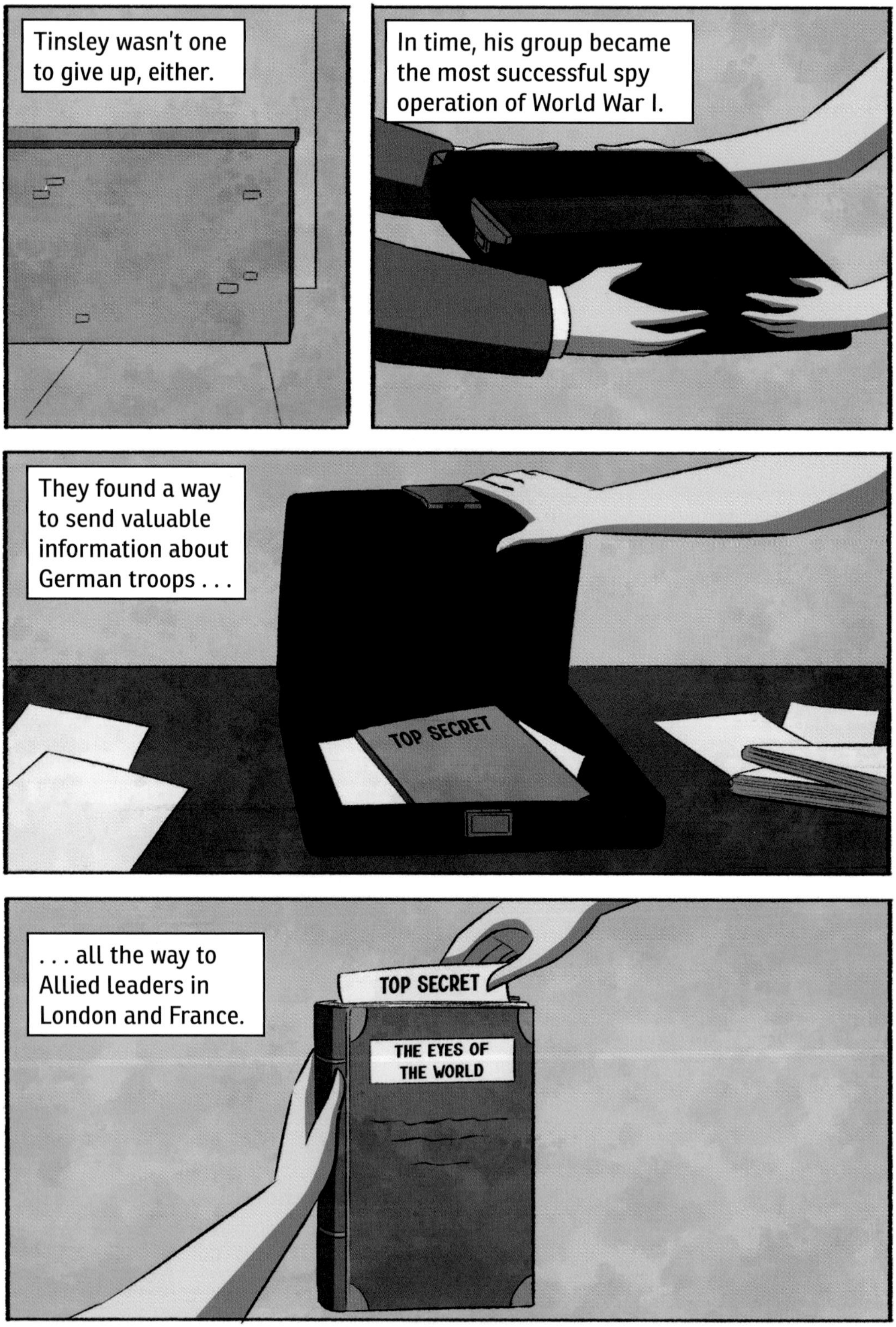
Tinsley wasn't one to give up, either.
In time, his group became the most successful spy operation of World War I.
They found a way to send valuable information about German troops . . .
TOP SECRET
. . . all the way to Allied leaders in London and France.
TOP SECRET
THE EYES OF THE WORLD

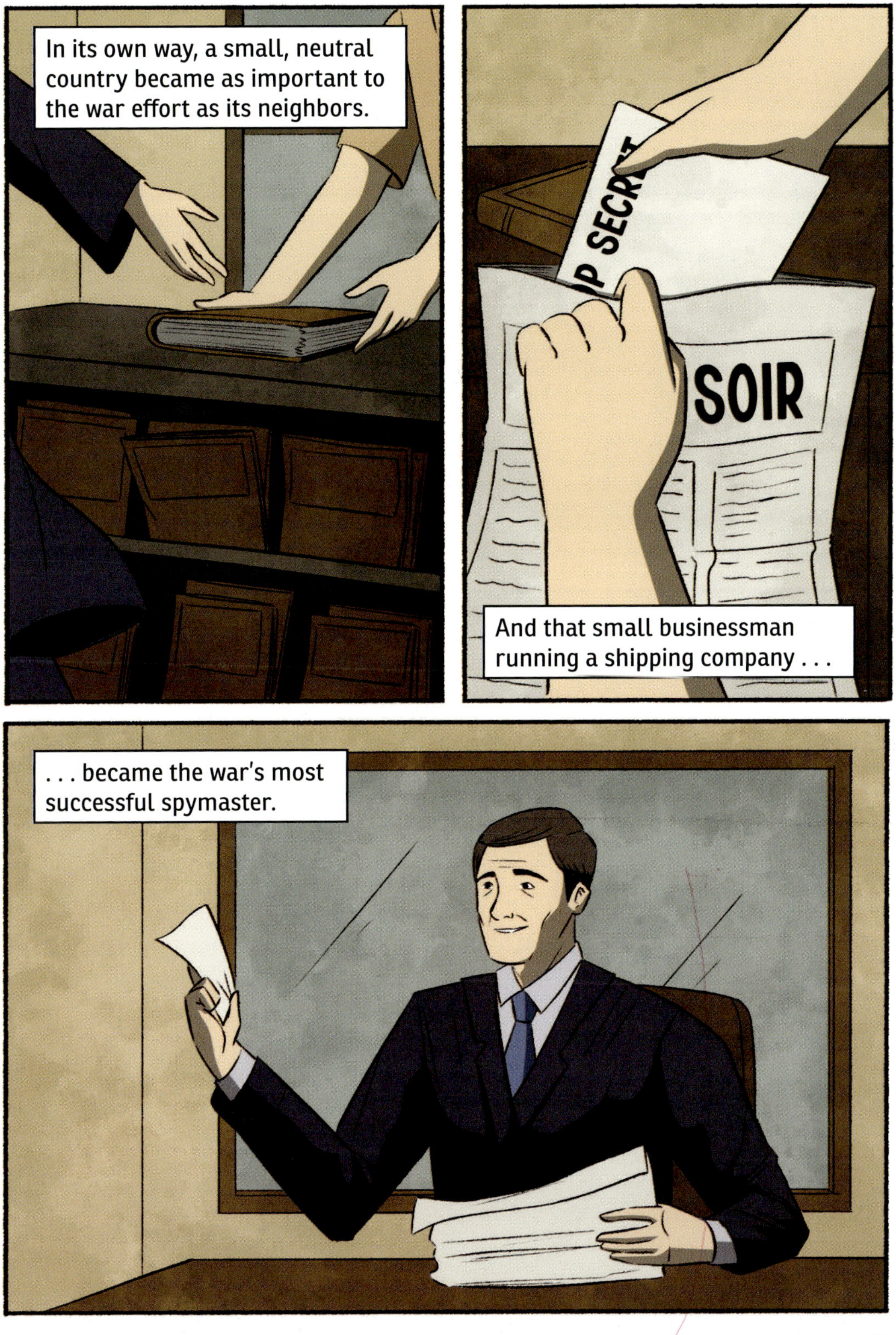

In its own way, a small, neutral country became as important to the war effort as its neighbors.
SOIR
And that small businessman running a shipping company . . .
. . . became the war's most successful spymaster.

CHAPTER THREE

SYLVANUS MORLEY: DIGGING FOR INFORMATION

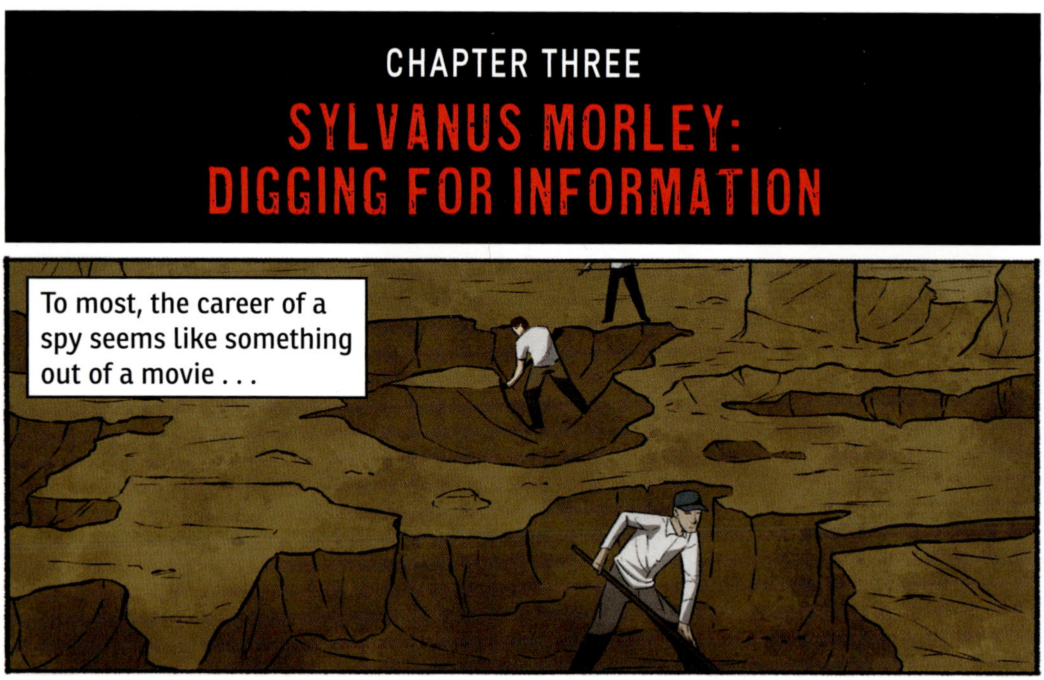
To most, the career of a spy seems like something out of a movie . . .

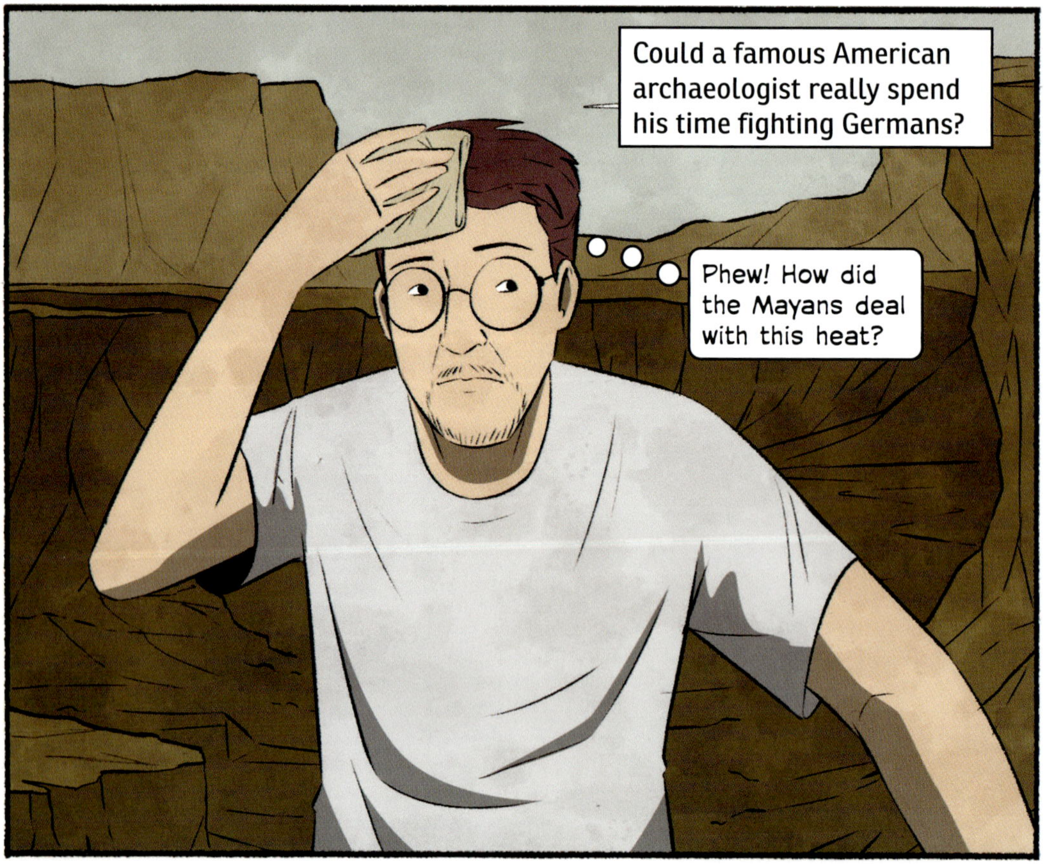
Could a famous American archaeologist really spend his time fighting Germans?
Phew! How did the Mayans deal with this heat?

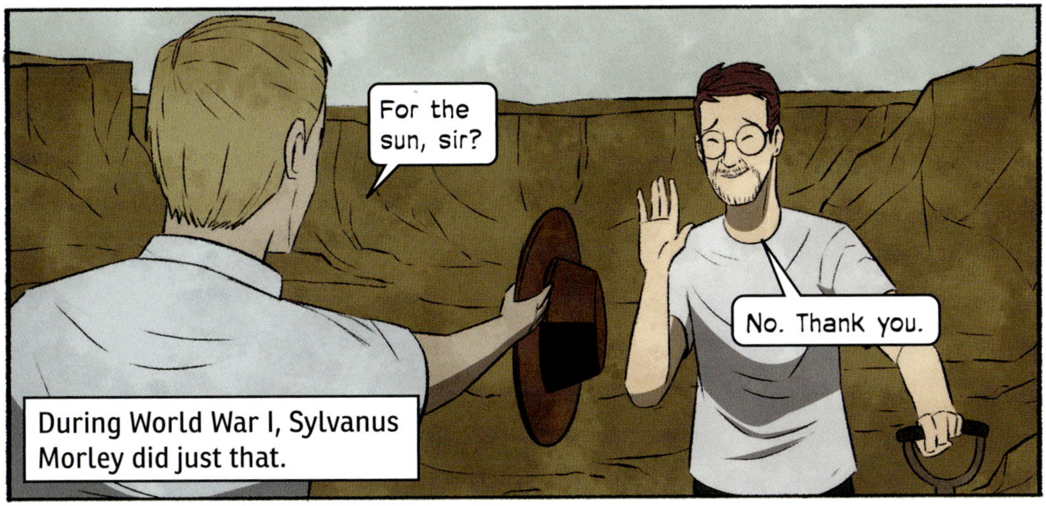
During World War I, Sylvanus Morley did just that.
For the sun, sir?
No. Thank you.

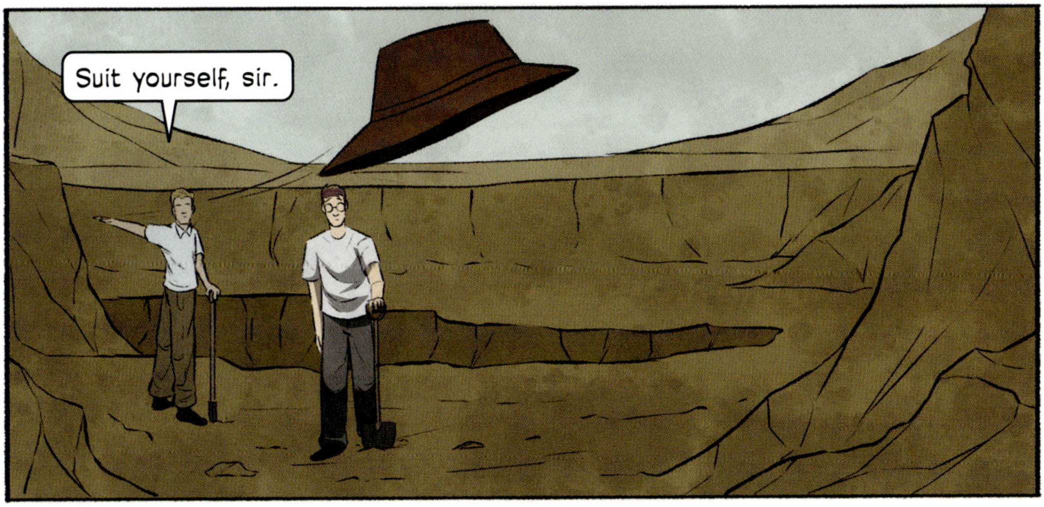
Suit yourself, sir.

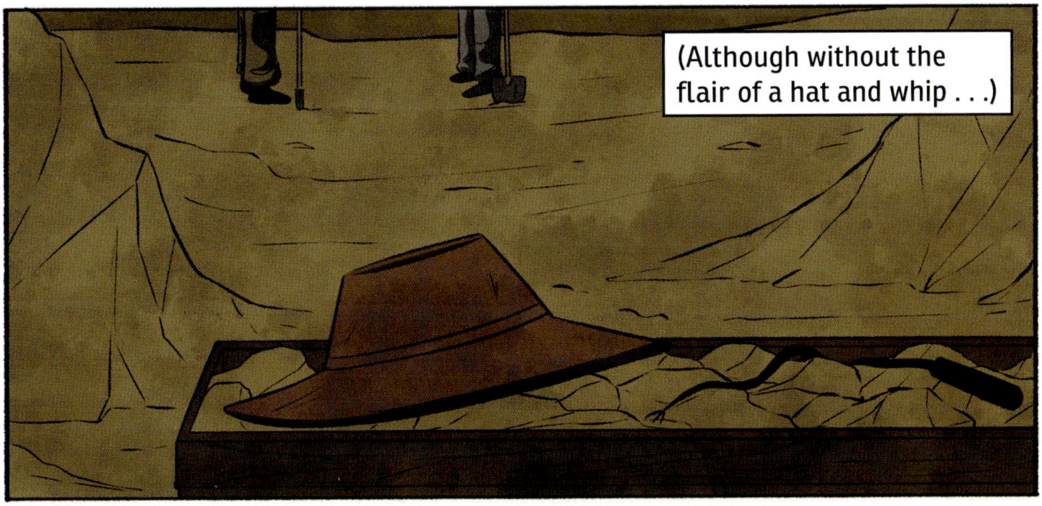
(Although without the flair of a hat and whip . . .)

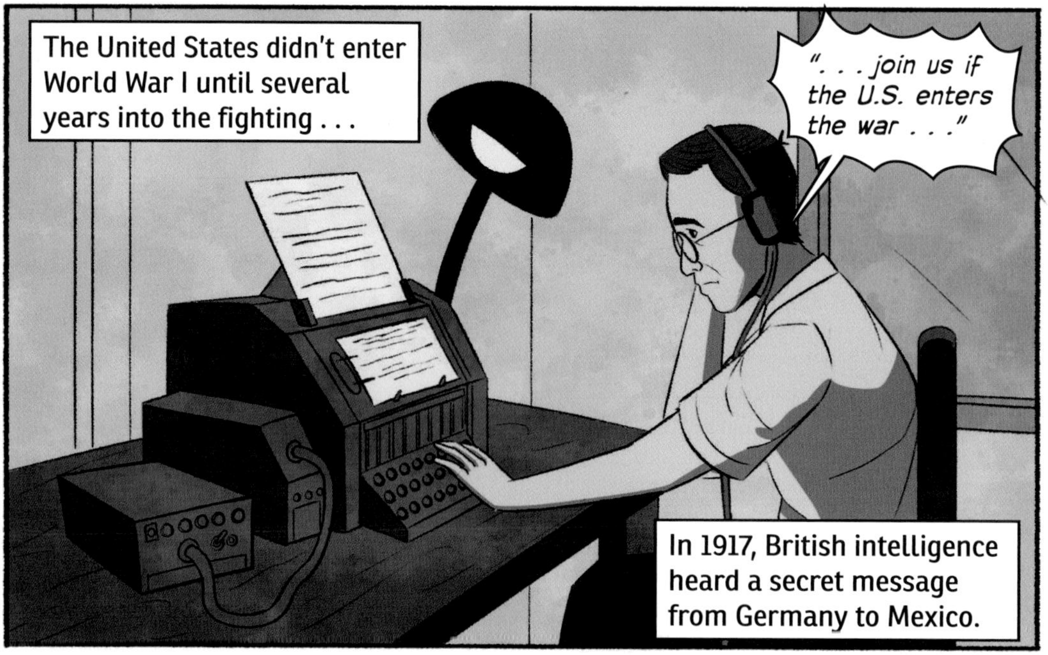
The United States didn't enter World War I until several years into the fighting . . .
". . . join us if the U.S. enters the war . . ."
In 1917, British intelligence heard a secret message from Germany to Mexico.

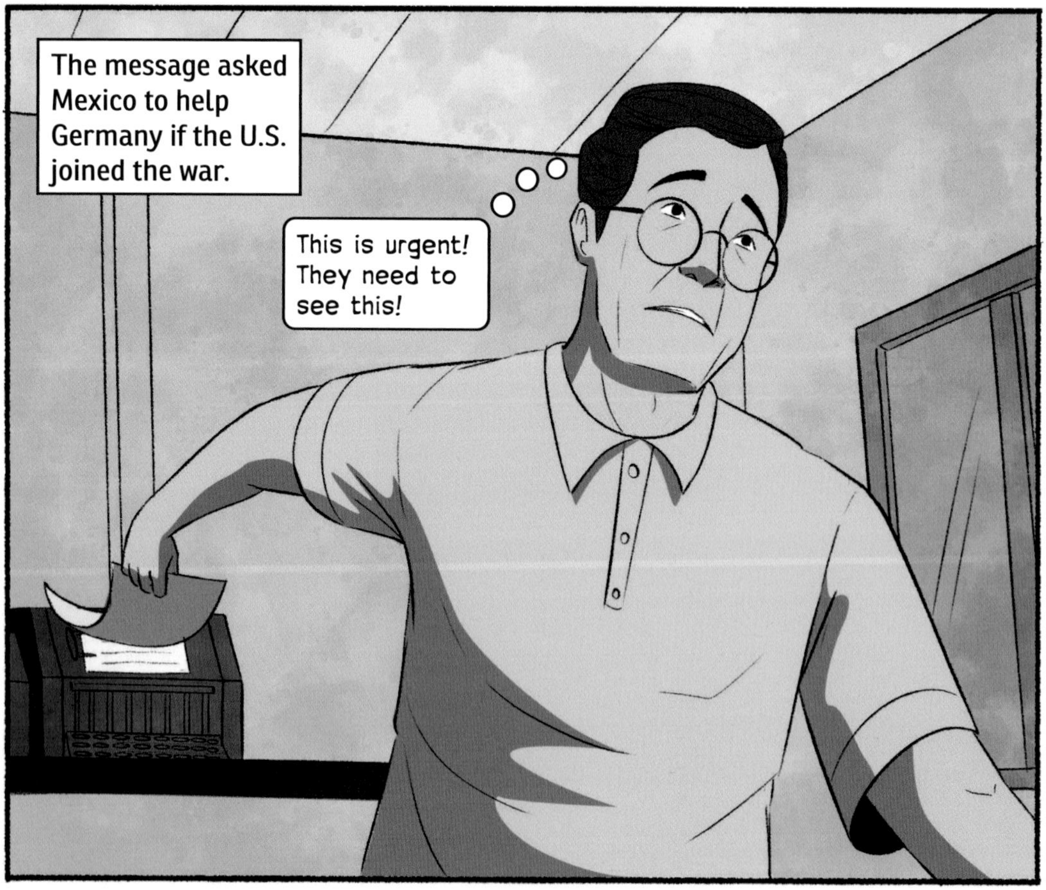
The message asked Mexico to help Germany if the U.S. joined the war.
This is urgent! They need to see this!

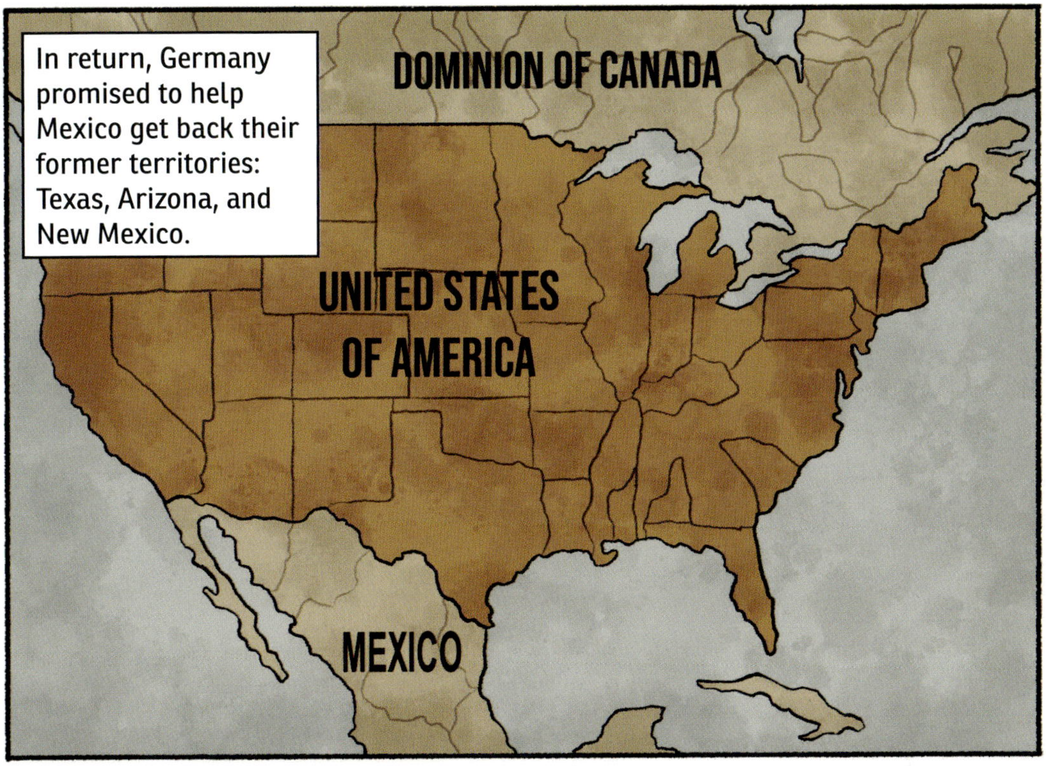
In return, Germany promised to help Mexico get back their former territories: Texas, Arizona, and New Mexico.
DOMINION OF CANADA
UNITED STATES OF AMERICA
MEXICO

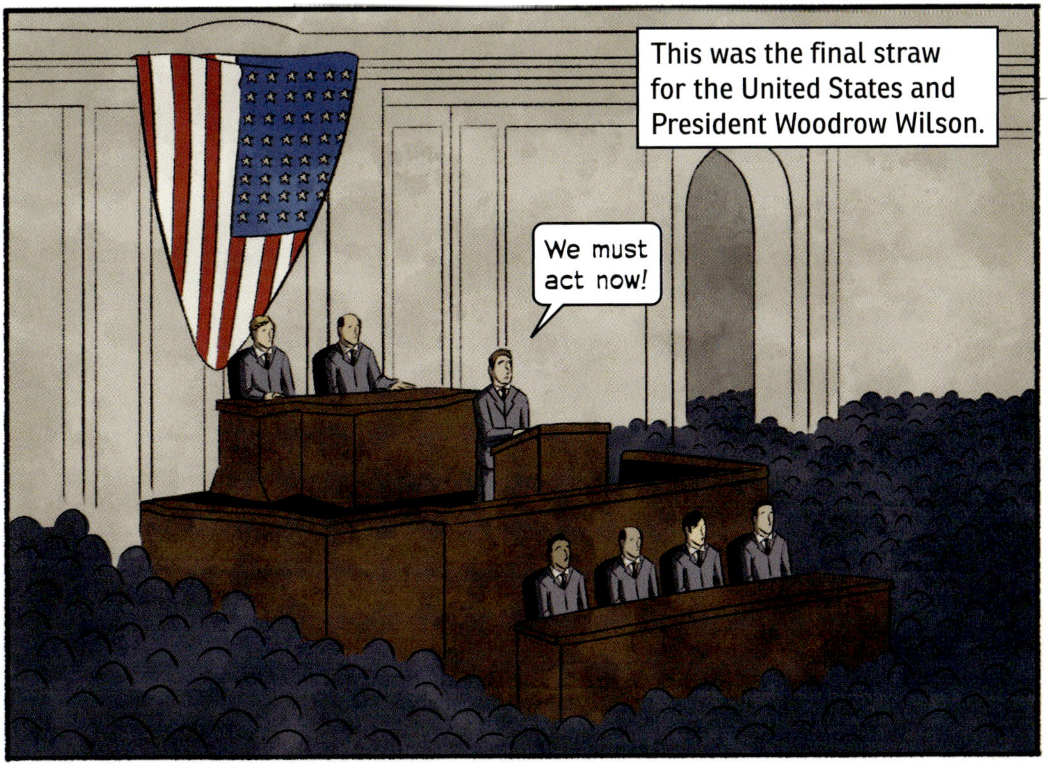
This was the final straw for the United States and President Woodrow Wilson.
We must act now!

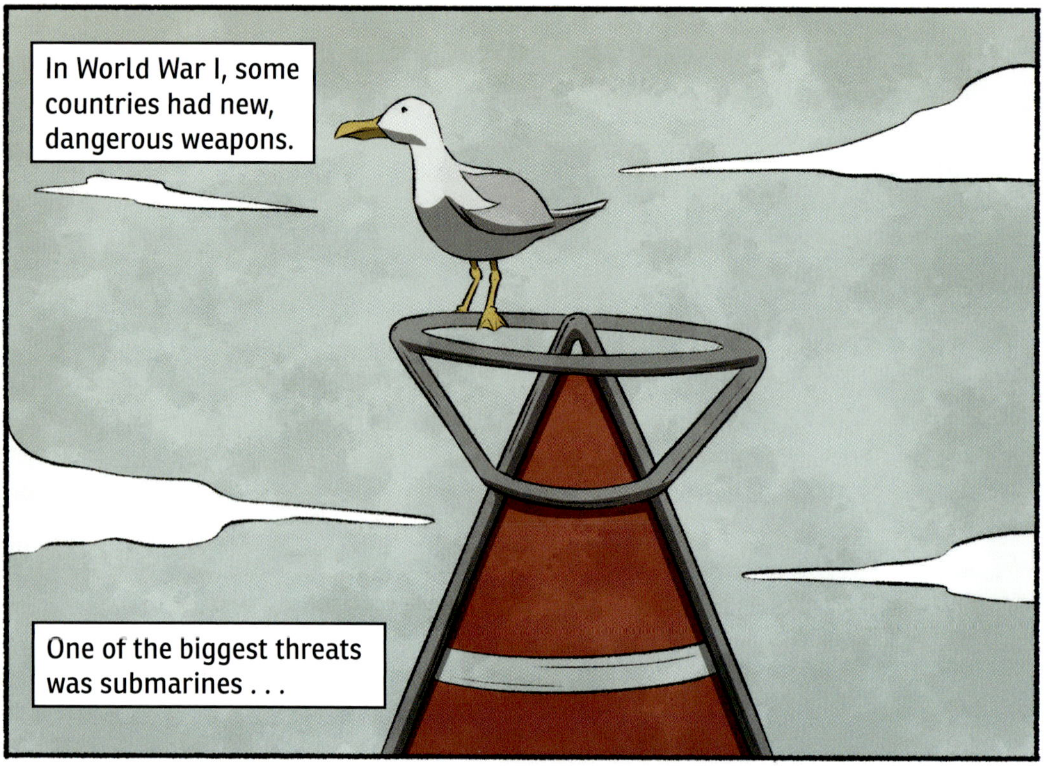
In World War I, some countries had new, dangerous weapons.
One of the biggest threats was submarines . . .

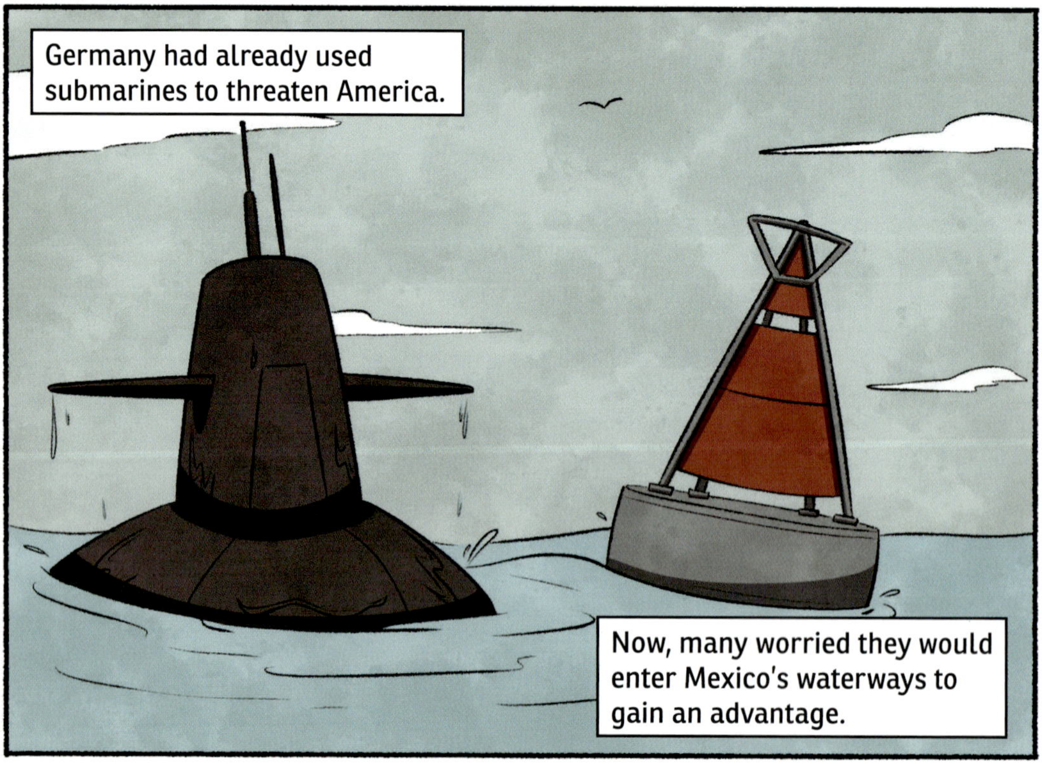
Germany had already used submarines to threaten America.
Now, many worried they would enter Mexico's waterways to gain an advantage.

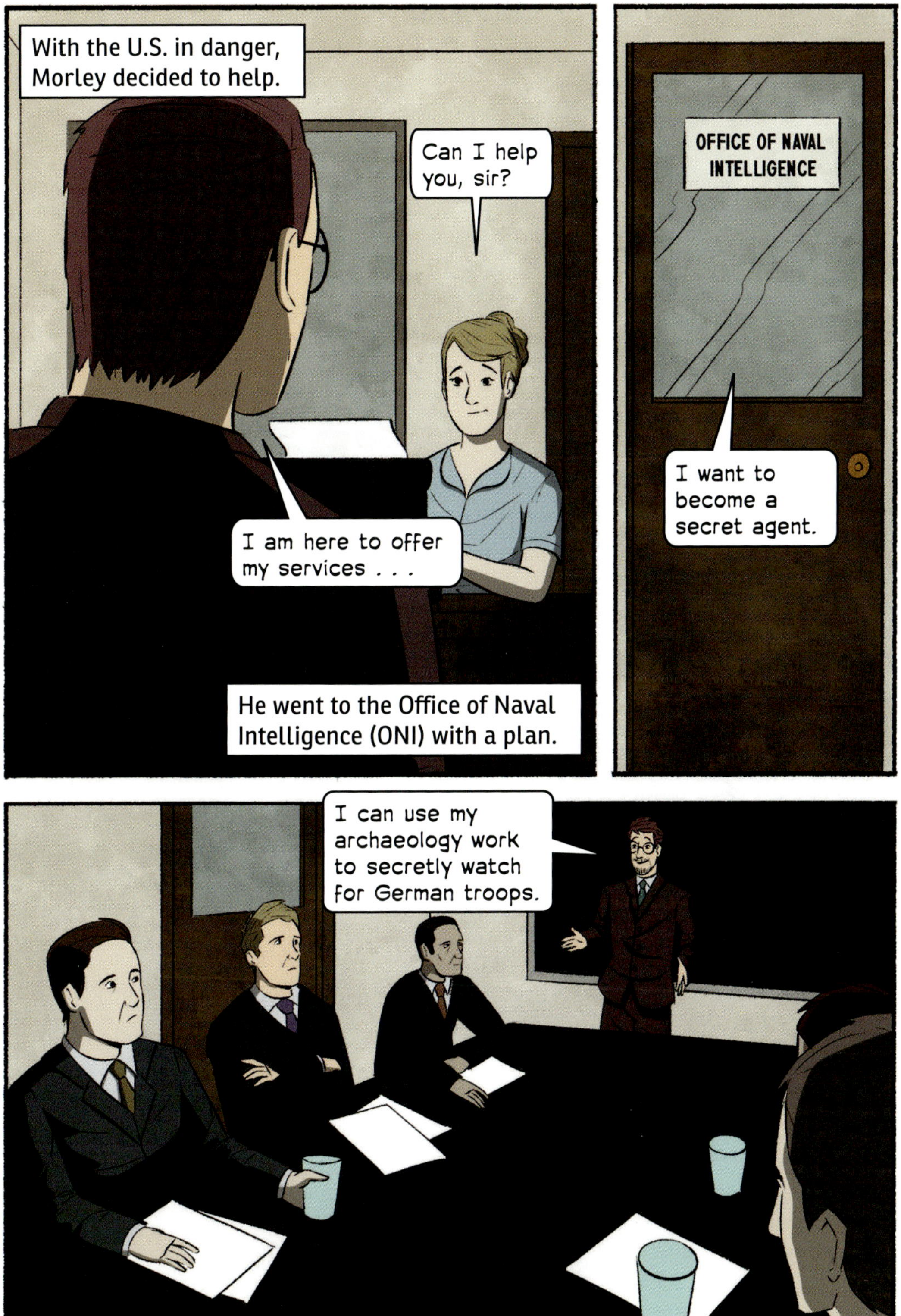
With the U.S. in danger, Morley decided to help.
Can I help you, sir?
I am here to offer my services . . .
He went to the Office of Naval Intelligence (ONI) with a plan.
OFFICE OF NAVAL INTELLIGENCE
I want to become a secret agent.
I can use my archaeology work to secretly watch for German troops.

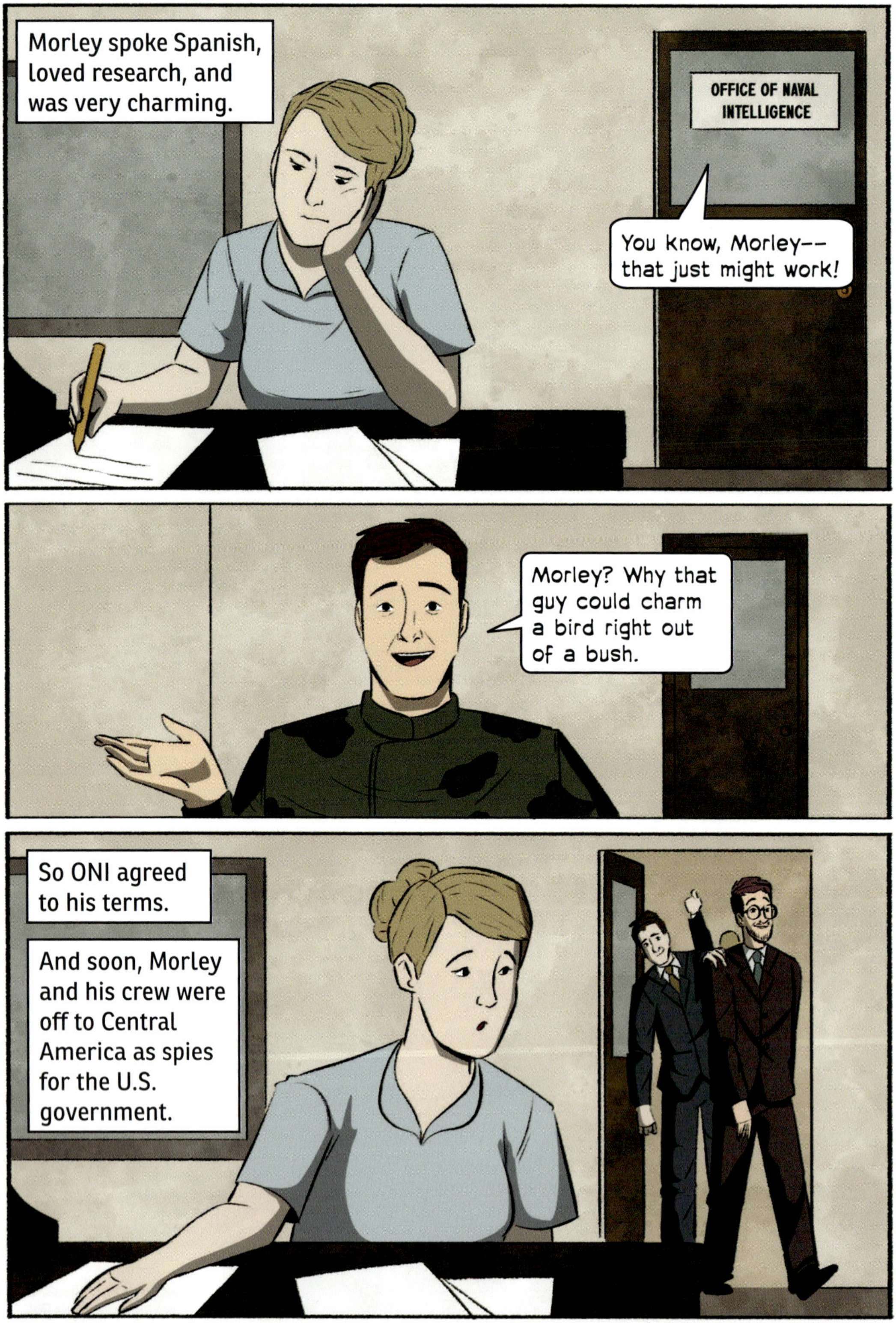

Morley spoke Spanish, loved research, and was very charming.
OFFICE OF NAVAL INTELLIGENCE
You know, Morley-- that just might work!
Morley? Why that guy could charm a bird right out of a bush.
So ONI agreed to his terms.
And soon, Morley and his crew were off to Central America as spies for the U.S. government.

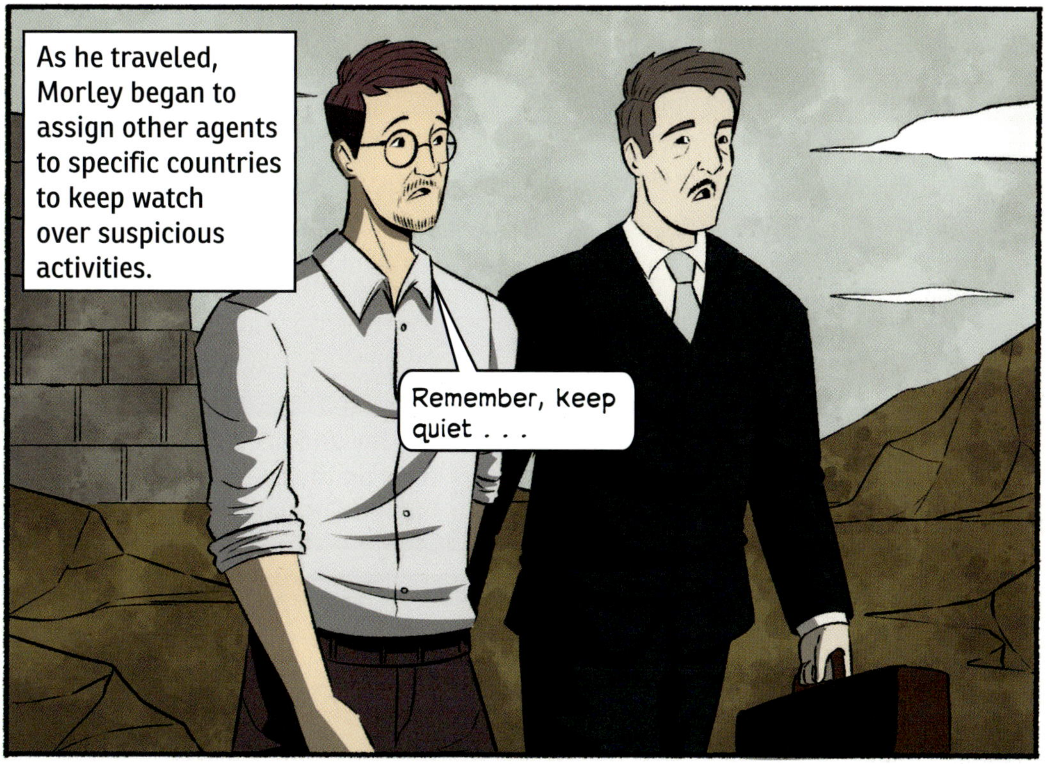
As he traveled, Morley began to assign other agents to specific countries to keep watch over suspicious activities.
Remember, keep quiet . . .

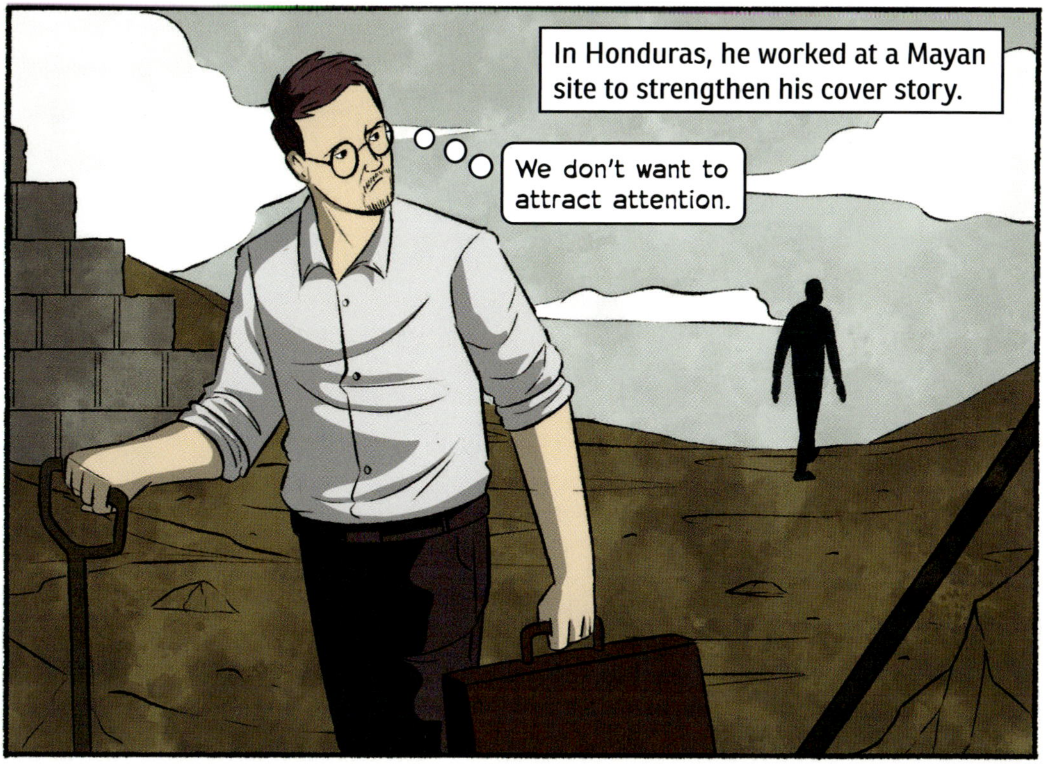
In Honduras, he worked at a Mayan site to strengthen his cover story.
We don't want to attract attention.

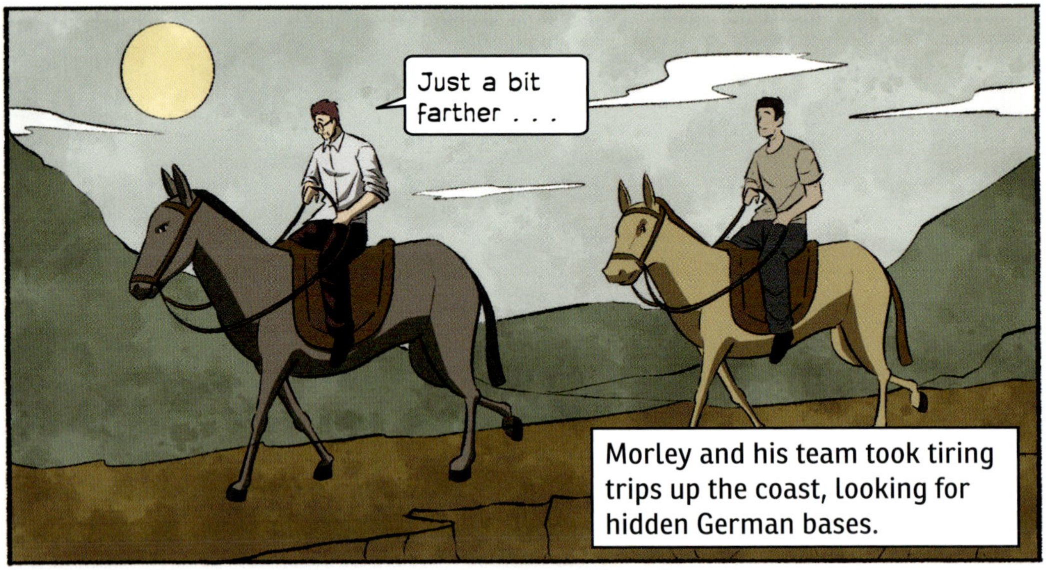
Just a bit farther . . .
Morley and his team took tiring trips up the coast, looking for hidden German bases.

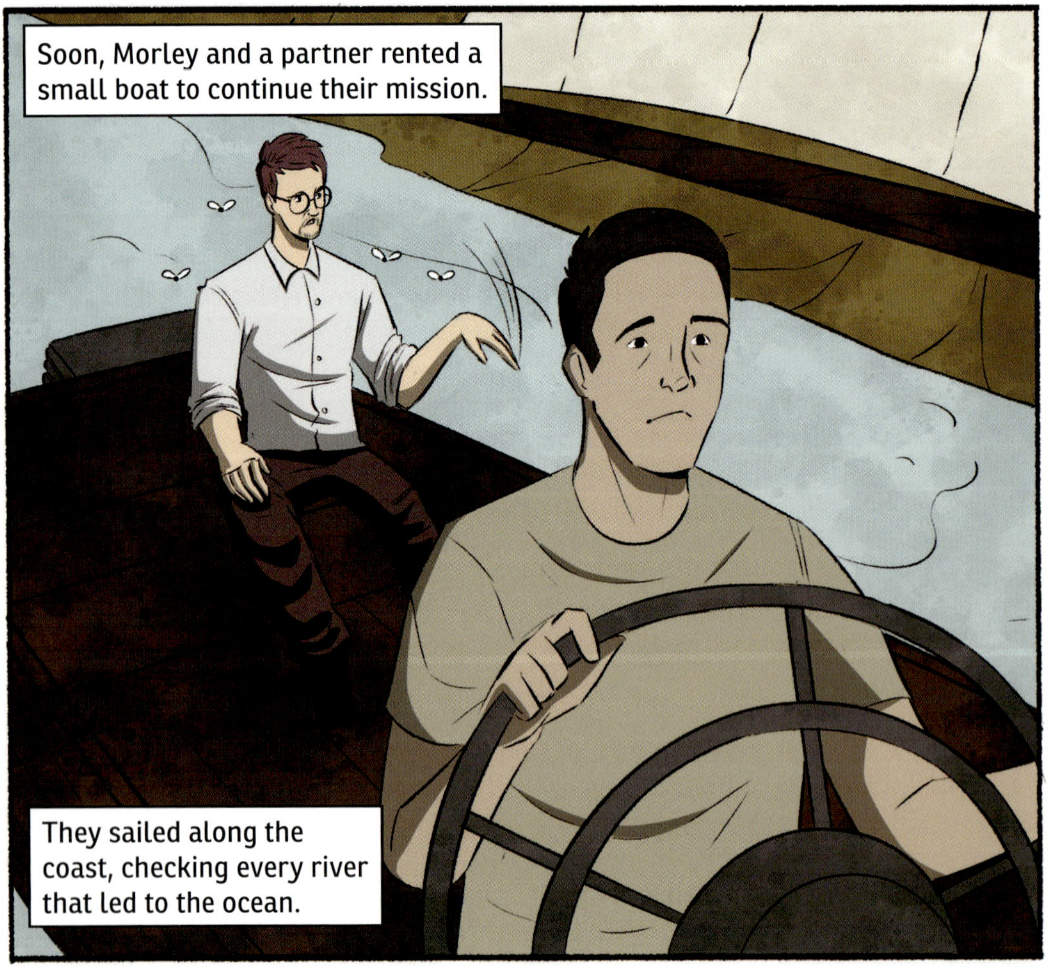
Soon, Morley and a partner rented a small boat to continue their mission.
They sailed along the coast, checking every river that led to the ocean.

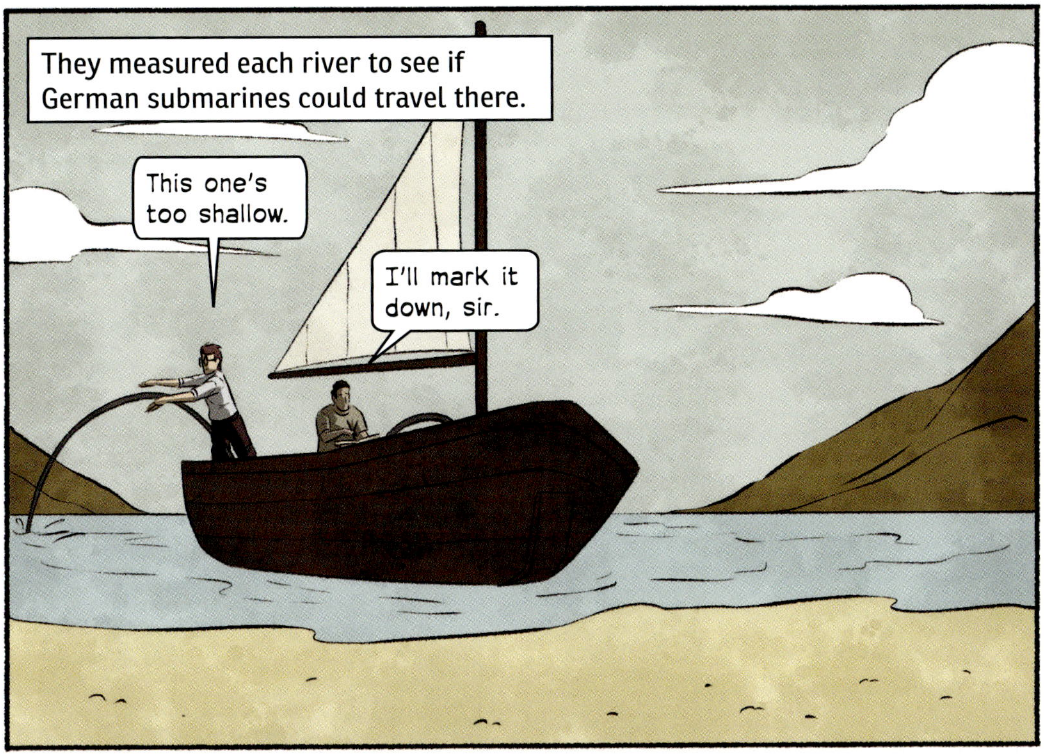
They measured each river to see if German submarines could travel there.
This one's too shallow.
I'll mark it down, sir.

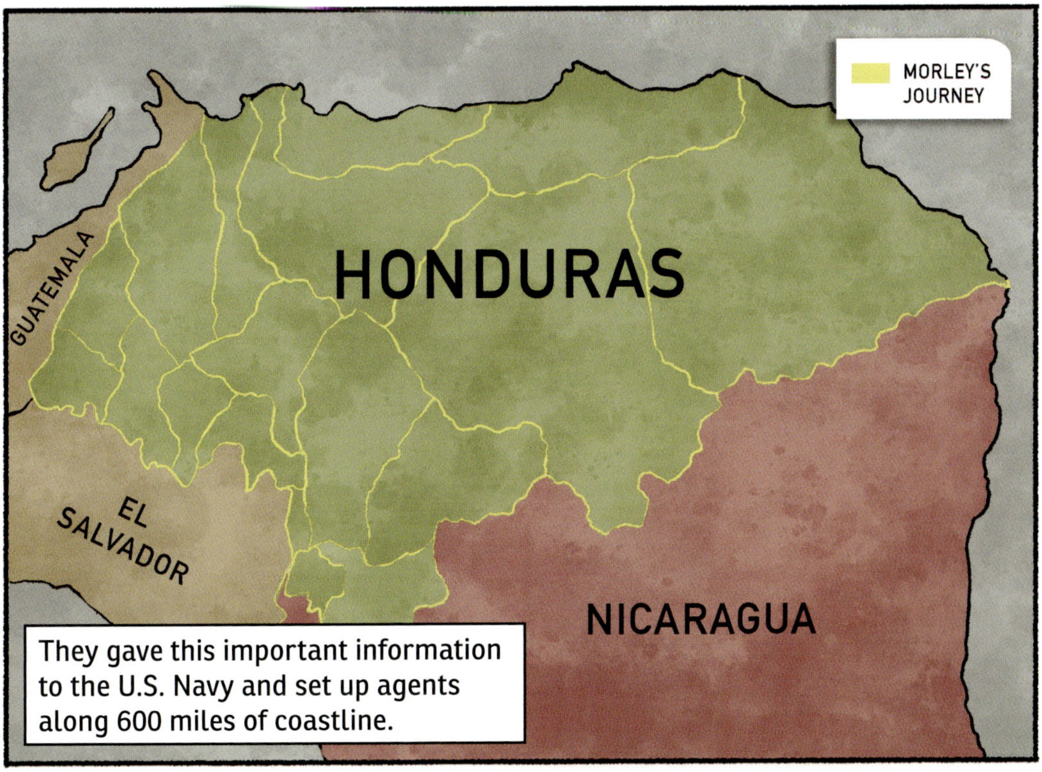
MORLEY'S JOURNEY
HONDURAS
GUATEMALA
EL SALVADOR
NICARAGUA
They gave this important information to the U.S. Navy and set up agents along 600 miles of coastline.

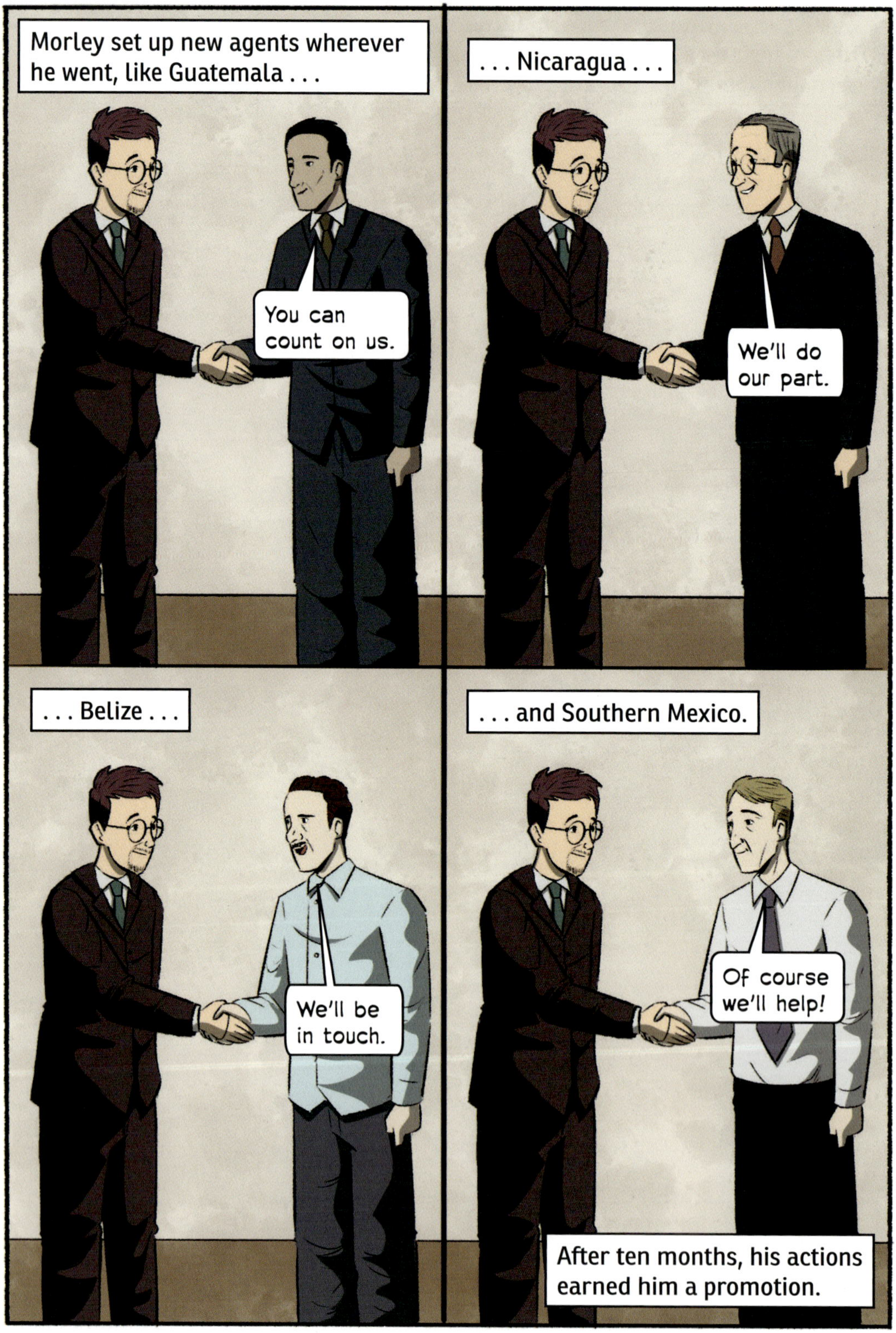
Morley set up new agents wherever he went, like Guatemala . . .
You can count on us.
. . . Nicaragua . . .
We'll do our part.
. . . Belize . . .
We'll be in touch.
. . . and Southern Mexico.
Of course we'll help!
After ten months, his actions earned him a promotion.

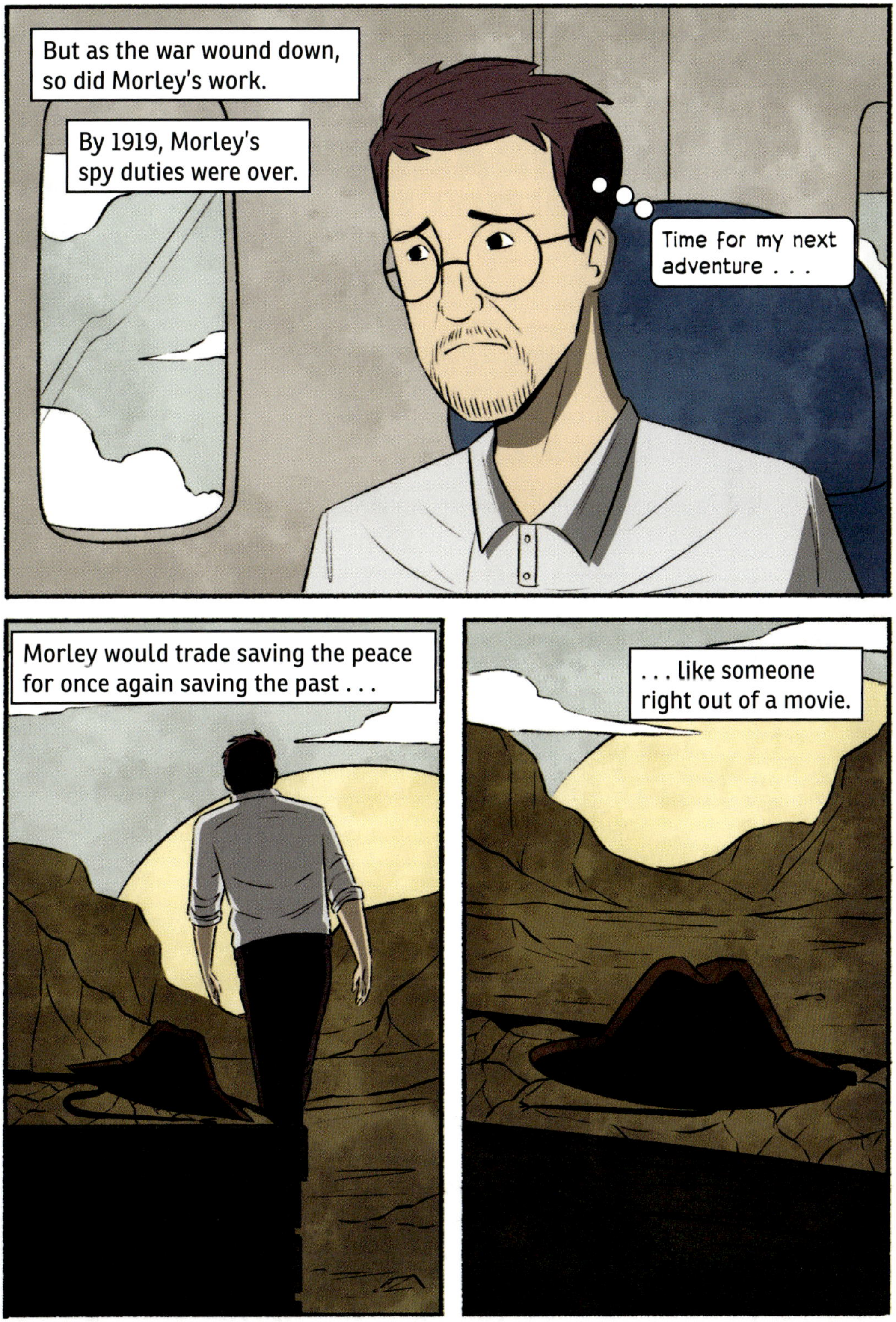
But as the war wound down, so did Morley's work.
By 1919, Morley's spy duties were over.
Time for my next adventure . . .
Morley would trade saving the peace for once again saving the past . . .
. . . like someone right out of a movie.

MORE ABOUT THE COURAGEOUS SPIES OF WORLD WAR I

- Louise de Bettignies traveled through Belgium and the Netherlands on her spy missions. She was eventually arrested while crossing the Franco-German border after returning from England.

- After her death, Louise de Bettignies was honored with the Légion d'Honneur, Croix de Guerre avec Palme, the British Military Medal, and was made an Officer of the Order of the British Empire

- One of Richard B. Tinsley's greatest achievements was getting military information from a German deserter. The deserter gave him a directory listing every unit in the German army, along with their positions.

- Richard B. Tinsley, considered the most important British spymaster of World War I, continued spying on Germany until he retired in 1923.

- Sylvanus Morley's background made him well-suited to chart enemy positions. He had a master's degree in archaeology and had also studied civil engineering, which gave him valuable mapping skills.

- Before joining the war effort, Sylvanus Morley was once mistaken for a Mexican revolutionary by Guatemalan soldiers. The soldiers shot and killed members of his expedition, an event that scarred Morley for life but didn't stop him from becoming a spy soon after.

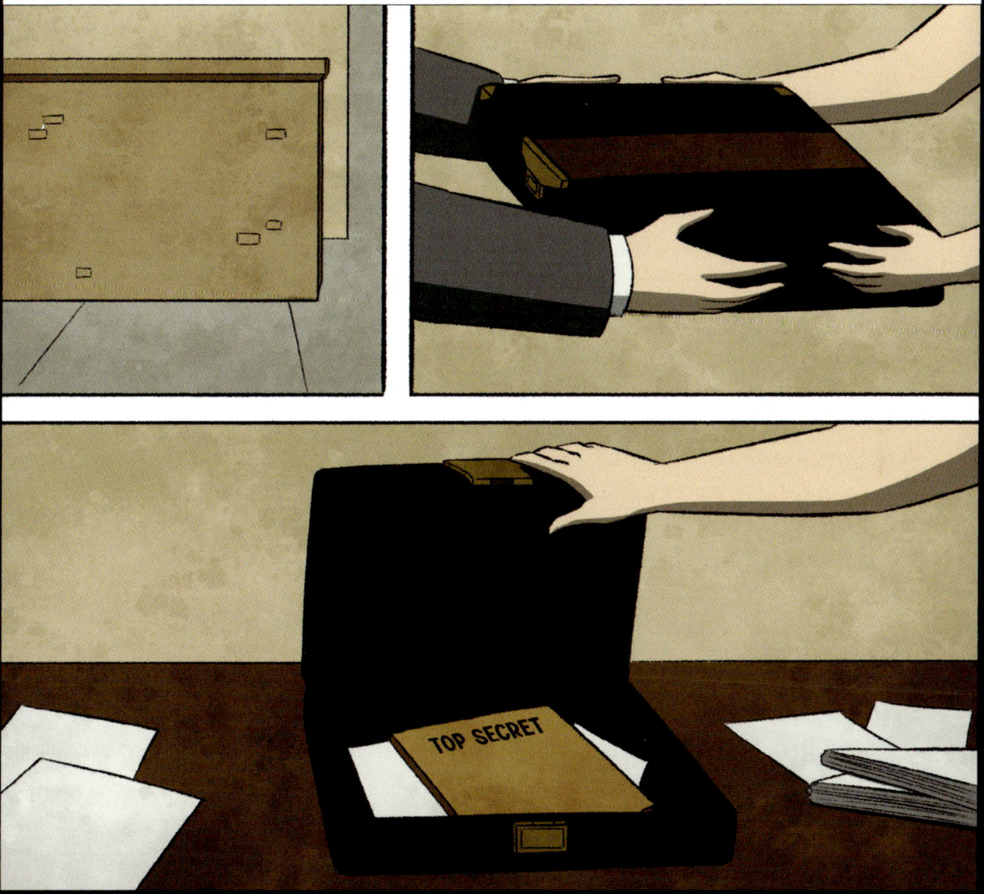
TOP SECRET

GLOSSARY

agent (AY-jent)—person who works for a government or organization to find out secrets

archaeologist (ar-kee-OL-uh-jist)—a person who studies old things buried in the ground to learn about the past

code name (COHD NAYM)—a name used to keep the real name of someone or something a secret

espionage (ES-pee-uh-naj)—being a spy or spying on others to find out secrets

mission (MISH-un)—an important job that someone is given to do

neutral (NOO-truhl)—not picking a side—like not choosing between two teams

submarine (SUB-muh-reen)—a ship that can go underwater

territory (TEHR-uh-tor-ee)—an area of land that belongs to a country or person

tutor (TOO-tur)—a person who has the responsibility of instructing and guiding another

READ MORE

Dickmann, Nancy. *The Horror of World War I*. North Mankato, MN: Capstone, 2018.

Lassieur, Allison. *Courageous Spies and International Intrigue of World War I*. North Mankato, MN: Capstone, 2017.

Yomtov, Nel. *Cher Ami Comes Through: Heroic Carrier Pigeon of World War I*. North Mankato, MN: Capstone, 2023.

INTERNET SITES

Imperial War Museums: 10 Ways Children Took Part In the First World War
iwm.org.uk/history/10-ways-children-took-part-in-the-first-world-war

The International Spy Museum
spymuseum.org

National Geographic Kids: World War 1 Facts
natgeokids.com/uk/discover/history/general-history/first-world-war

ABOUT THE AUTHOR

PHOTO COURTESY OF
DOROTHY MANNING PHOTOGRAPHY

Matthew K. Manning is the author of more than 100 books and just as many comic books. Some of his favorite projects include the popular comic book crossover Batman/Teenage Mutant Ninja Turtles Adventures and the twelve-issue series Marvel Action: Avengers for IDW, *Exploring Gotham City* for Insight Editions, and the six-volume chapter book series Xander and the Rainbow-Barfing Unicorns for Capstone. Manning lives in Asheville, North Carolina, with his wife, Dorothy, and their two kids, Lilly and Gwen.

ABOUT THE ILLUSTRATOR

PHOTO COURTESY
OF LEO TRINIDAD

Leo Trinidad is a *New York Times* bestselling illustrator and animator from Costa Rica. For more than fifteen years, he's been creating content for children's books and TV shows. His short form series have aired in more than forty territories around the world on channels like Disney and Cartoon Network.